EURO Advanced Tutorials on Operational Research

Series Editors

M. Grazia Speranza, Brescia, Italy
José Fernando Oliveira, Porto, Portugal

More information about this series at http://www.springer.com/series/13840

Abraham Duarte · Manuel Laguna
Rafael Martí

Metaheuristics for Business Analytics

A Decision Modeling Approach

Springer

Abraham Duarte
E.T.S. Ingeniería Informática
Universidad Rey Juan Carlos
Madrid
Spain

Rafael Martí
Universidad de Valencia
Burjassot, Valencia
Spain

Manuel Laguna
Leeds School of Business
Boulder, CO
USA

ISSN 2364-687X ISSN 2364-6888 (electronic)
EURO Advanced Tutorials on Operational Research
ISBN 978-3-319-68117-7 ISBN 978-3-319-68119-1 (eBook)
https://doi.org/10.1007/978-3-319-68119-1

Library of Congress Control Number: 2017953784

Printed on acid-free paper

This Springer imprint is published by Springer Nature
The registered company is Springer International Publishing AG
The registered company address is: Gewerbestrasse 11, 6330 Cham, Switzerland

A mi chica de ayer.

Rafa Martí

Preface

Business Analytics (BA) focuses on identifying and leveraging business opportunities. BA is based on a decision-analysis process that uses data, computers, statistics, and mathematics to solve business problems. BA can be basically defined as the science of making better decisions.

Some well-known and often studied decision modeling methods often encounter a great deal of difficulty when faced with the challenge of solving hard problems related to predictive and prescriptive analytics that abound in the real world. Vitally important applications not only in business, but also in engineering, economics, and science cannot be tackled with any reasonable hope of success, within practical time horizons, by solution methods that have been the predominant focus of academic research throughout the past three decades (and which are still the focus of many textbooks). The metaheuristic approaches are dramatically changing our ability to solve problems of practical significance and are extending the frontier of problems that can be handled effectively, yielding solutions whose quality often significantly surpasses that obtained by methods previously applied.

Spreadsheet packages provide a popular way to first build decision models of business problems, and then solve them. Unfortunately, the main solution tools within popular electronic spreadsheet software such as Microsoft Excel are based on the so-called classical methods that include linear programming, branch and bound, or interior point methods. Tools based on metaheuristics technology are for the most part ignored or poorly executed. This is why when practitioners need to solve real-world business problems, they often experience frustration with the techniques that are available in the environment that is most familiar them, namely electronic spreadsheets. The limitations are not only on the size of problems that they are able to solve but also on the real-life complexities that they are able to include in their models.

This book's goal is to provide the basic principles and fundamental ideas that will allow master-level business students to create valuable applications based on metaheuristic technologies. The book includes the Visual Basic for Excel source code of the procedures introduced in each chapter. The code, in most cases, is meant as an illustration on how to create solution procedures for a variety of problems. The modular design of the code allows students to piece together solutions to new problems that they will encounter in practice or as end-of-the-chapter exercises. As the goal of this book series states, this book is meant to fill the gap between traditional textbooks and research papers. Traditional textbooks in business analytics and decision modeling focus on showing how the so-called classical optimization methods can be used to find solutions to business problems, while research papers in the metaheuristic literature focus on development of techniques and pay little attention to the business problems that these procedures could tackle. Additionally, the implementation of metaheuristic methods in research articles is usually accomplished with general-purpose languages that are meant for commercial applications, such as C++ or Java, and which are incomprehensible to those without computer programming expertise. This book shows not only how to model a business problem on a spreadsheet but also how to design and create a Visual Basic application in Excel based on metaheuristic principles.

Madrid, Spain Abraham Duarte
Boulder, USA Manuel Laguna
Valencia, Spain Rafael Martí
July 2017

Contents

Chapter 1
Introduction to Spreadsheet Modeling and Metaheuristics

Models, as a simplified representation of reality, are used daily in an attempt to control or understand some aspects of a real system. Simplification of reality is the accepted view of the modeling process, which assumes that reality represents the absolute truth. Without getting too deep into a philosophical discourse, it is worth mentioning the notion of model-dependent realism, a phrase coined by physicists Stephen Hawkings and Leonard Molinow in their book The Grand Design. Model-dependent realism "is based on the idea that our brains interpret the input from our sensory organs by making a model of the world to aid in the decision-making process." This implies that more than one model of a real system can be built and that we are free to use whatever model is more convenient as long as it has the same accuracy as other alternative models. It also implies that there is no theory-independent concept of reality. Therefore, "according to model-dependent realism, it is pointless to ask whether a model is real, only whether it agrees with observation." Hawkings and Molinow consider that a good model:

is elegant,
contains few arbitrary or adjustable elements,
agrees with and explains all existing observations, and
makes detailed predictions about future observations.

While these characteristics are mentioned in the context of models to explain physical phenomena such as the creation of the universe, they seem to apply to the general modeling process. Clearly, the first characteristic (i.e., elegance) is subjective and hard to measure. However, it is closely related to the second one. In Chap. 2, we will discuss the elements of solution methods and we will give specific examples of the concept of elegance as it relates to the number of arbitrary of adjustable parameters. In some sense, elegance is related to simplicity, and to paraphrase Einstein, a model should be as simple as possible but not simpler. We will come back to this idea later in the book.

A. Duarte et al., *Metaheuristics for Business Analytics*, EURO Advanced Tutorials on Operational Research, https://doi.org/10.1007/978-3-319-68119-1_1

We focus now the discussion back to the modeling process in the context of business analytics (BA). The problems faced by decision makers in today's competitive business environment are often extremely complex and can be addressed by numerous possible courses of action. Evaluating these alternatives and gaining insight from past performance is the essence of business analytics. BA considers the extensive use of data, methods and fact-based management to support and improve decision making. While business intelligence focuses on data handling, queries and reports to discover patterns and generate information associated with products, services and customers, business analytics uses data and models to explain the performance of a business and how it can be improved.

BA models can help at the strategic level, for instance, on decisions about acquisitions and expansions. They can also be applied to improve tactical decisions, such as those related to production and employee scheduling, vehicle routing, and product mixes. Depending on the application, models may be embedded in complex information systems (e.g., as part of Enterprise Resource Planning software) or they may be implemented separately as a standalone decision-support system. Spreadsheets have become a common platform for the development of these standalone business models because they provide the analyst with integrated analytical tools and remarkable flexibility to customize and build additional functionality. The focus of this book is on building spreadsheet models as decision-making tools for business analytics. The enhanced functionality of the models we build is provided by the application of metaheuristic technology. To this end, we use Microsoft Excel as our implementation platform and Visual Basic for Applications as the programming environment that is needed for the metaheuristic implementations.

There are several types of models with various degrees of complexity [7]. The most basic and informal are **mental models**, which we create in our heads and allow us to make quick decisions. A golfer creates a mental model when selecting a club for his approach shot by taking into consideration distance, wind, hazards, and green elevation. **Visual models** add a layer of formality over mental models and consist of graphics or diagrams to represent real entities or situations. For example, an organizational chart depicts reporting lines in an organization and unveils communication channels. **Physical models** are objects that represent either other objects or concepts, such as an architect's scale model of a new building or an automotive designer's scale model of a new automobile. **Mathematical models** consist of equations and relationships among quantities and variables to represent situations in business (Markowitz model for portfolio selection), science (Feynmans relativistic chessboard model), engineering (Navier–Stokes equations), and public policy (Forrester's system dynamics). Most of the concepts in this book are illustrated through the use of mathematical models. We view **spreadsheet models** as a means for implementing mathematical models.

The model types mentioned above have some obvious differences but they also have a set of common elements. First, building a model is motivated by the need to make a decision, for example, a golfer that must decide which golf club to choose for an approach shot, or a store manager that needs to make a decision about how many jackets of each style, brand, color, and size to order to satisfy the unknown demand of an upcoming ski season. Second, all models consider controllable and uncontrollable inputs that are related to the decision that needs to be made. Controllable inputs are also referred to as **decision variables** because they represent quantities or factors that a decision maker can control and change (typically within limits). For example, in the golfing example, the golfer can control the swing speed, which in turn affects his club selection. However, the golfer has no control over the wind, which also affects the selection of the most appropriate club to hit. Likewise, a store manager can choose how many jackets to order but has no control over the quality and the length of the ski season, as determined by the amount of snowfall. Uncontrollable inputs are referred as **parameters** and although they affect the decision-making process, the decision maker has no direct control over them. Parameters are typically estimated and varied to perform what-if analyses. In most cases, the interaction of the inputs produce **constraints** that limit the feasibility of the decisions. For instance, space and/or budget limitations may restrict the number of jackets of each type that the store manager can order.

All models have outputs. An **output** is a quantity or result that the model is predicting will occur considering the values of all inputs. Models typically generate more than one outcome. For instance, in the ski jacket ordering example, a model can predict total inventory cost (i.e., cost of ordering plus the cost of holding the inventory) and it could also estimate the out-stock probability (by making some assumptions about the ski season and its relation to the demand for each type of jacket). In mathematical modeling, one or more outputs are used to formulate **objective functions**, for instance, to minimize total cost. While primary outputs are included in the formulation of objective functions, secondary outputs are useful for setting additional constraints. For instance, the store manager might want to minimize total cost, but would like to do so while not exceeding a given probability of running out of stock. Note that a trivial way of minimizing inventory costs is by not ordering anything, which results in no ordering cost and no holding cost. However, this decision is not feasible if a limit on the out-stock probability is imposed.

Clearly, models transform inputs into outputs. In the golfing example, the golfer mentally processes the inputs, "estimates" the outputs, and then makes a decision. In the ski jacket situation, the store manager could use the mathematical relationships among the input quantities to calculate the total cost. Then he/she could consider different possible order quantities and choose the one that produces the least total cost while not exceeding the desired out-stock probability. The transformation of inputs into outputs has a very specific structure that determines the purpose of the model. Figure 1.1 shows a simple graphical representation of a model that transforms inputs (parameters and decision variables) into outputs by establishing mathematical relationships with spreadsheet formulas.

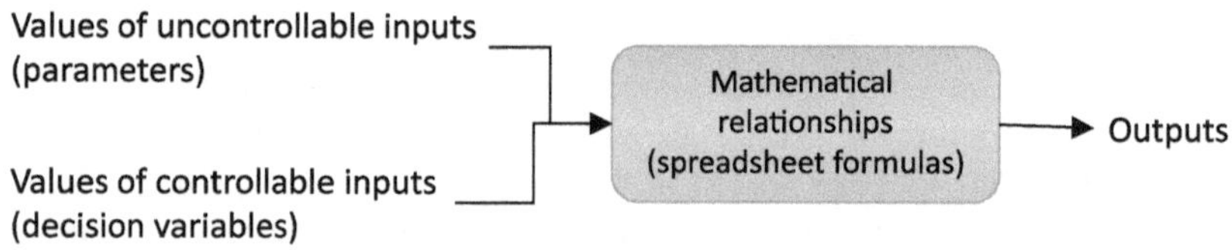

Fig. 1.1 Graphical view of a mathematical model

The purpose of the mathematical models that we discuss in this book is improving decision making in the area of business analytics. There are three classes of business analytics models: descriptive, predictive, and prescriptive [1]. **Descriptive models** use historical data to help the analyst understand past and current business performance and make informed decisions. These models are the most popular and the best understood. Descriptive models help characterize, classify, and aggregate data to turn it into useful information that can be the basis for measuring business performance. Typical outcomes include charts and reports of sales, revenue, and cost. Customized reports allow analysts to make queries about the penetration rate of an advertising campaign or the turnover ratio of critical inventories. Typical questions that descriptive models help to answer include: What is the regional demand profile of a set of products? What is the variation of the production cost in the last 8 quarters? Descriptive models include data visualization and exploration, descriptive statistics, sampling and estimation, and statistical inference.

Predictive models analyze past and current data in an effort to predict future performance, by detecting patterns and/or relationships among data attributes and parameters. For instance, a store manager might want to predict the demand for ski-wear of different colors and sizes for the next ski season. Predictive models are also use to assess risk. For example, a model that predicts sales can be used to assess the risk of running out of stock for a given ordering policy. A banker could use historical data to identify loan applicants that might default or to alert credit card holders of possible fraudulent charges. Predictive models help provide insight on questions such as: What is the estimated probability of losing money on a new product line? What level of customer service should we expect with a given workforce? Predictive models include regression analysis, forecasting, simulation, and data mining.

Prescriptive models use input data and functional relationships to create mathematical formulations in order to optimize one or more outputs. The optimization process consists of minimizing or maximizing an objective function. Typical objectives include the maximization of profit or minimization of cost. For instance, an airline might want to determine how to set ticket prices in order to maximize revenue. A telecommunications company might want to know where to locate mobile-phone towers in order to minimize cost while providing a specified amount of coverage in a region. The questions that prescriptive models address include: What investments should be selected to maximize expected revenue while not exceeding a specified limit on risk? How should delivery vehicles be routed in order to minimize total delivery cost? Note that predictive models could be embedded in prescriptive models in order to deal with uncertainty and be able to assess risk. Prescriptive models include linear, integer, and nonlinear programming, simulation-optimization, and metaheuristics.

1.1 Spreadsheet Engineering

Spreadsheet engineering is the application of software engineering principles to spreadsheets with the goals of increasing the productivity of spreadsheet programmers, decreasing the frequency and severity of spreadsheet errors, enhancing spreadsheet maintainability, and increasing the number of spreadsheet implementations performed by end users [4]. A spreadsheet might be considered a rapid development language to program computers. More than 50 years of computer programming has produced important software engineering principles that are both platform and language independent and hence apply to spreadsheet development. For instance, advanced planning (i.e., designing before programming) is one of the most important principles in order to build well-engineered spreadsheets. Planning not only reduces the overall time required to perform spreadsheet analysis but also avoids "spaghetti" coding and logic (i.e., lack of modular structure). Adopting software engineering principles and techniques help spreadsheet designers avoid flaws such as commingling of data and calculations as well as inadequate code documentation.

As mentioned by [5], for business analysts to benefit from spreadsheet modeling, they need to be able to quickly create spreadsheets that accurately express their business knowledge in a way that can be understood by other people. In other words, the spreadsheet modeling process must be effective, efficient, and must result in transferable models:

- **Effectiveness**. An effective process results in models that meet the analysts specifications. This means that the resulting models accurately capture the essence of the business situation.
- **Efficiency**. An effective design process achieves the desired results with minimum time and effort. Business analysts have limited time, as dictated by deadlines. Spreadsheet models must be created quickly, with minimal wasted effort, rework, and debugging.
- **Transferability**. Many crucial spreadsheets are not limited to personal use and they become important organizational assets and productivity tools. Therefore, spreadsheet models must be well-documented so they can be understood by people other than the developer.

Spreadsheet engineering suggests that there are three phases associated with developing an error-free spreadsheet model: designing, building, and testing. While many spreadsheet users assume that spreadsheet models are error-free, this seems to be very far from reality. Consider, for example, these two "horror stories" reported by the European Spreadsheet Risk Interest Group (EuSpRiG)[1]:

> A January 16, 2013 report by JP Morgan states that "... further errors were discovered in the Basel II.5 model, including, most significantly, an operational error in the calculation of the relative changes in hazard rates and correlation estimates. Specifically, after subtracting the old rate from the new rate, the spreadsheet divided by their sum instead of their average, as the modeler had intended. This error likely had the effect of muting volatility by a factor of two and of lowering the VaR.[2]"

> In their 2010 paper "Growth in a Time of Debt," economists Carmen Reinhart (University of Maryland) and Kenneth S. Rogoff (Harvard University) conclude that when government debt exceeds 90 percent of GDP "median growth rates fall by one percent, and average growth falls considerably more". This conclusion was widely cited during the recent great recession and provided the intellectual foundation for the austerity measures implemented around the world. However, a group of University of Massachusetts students, unable to reproduce the results, obtained Reinhart and Rogoffs spreadsheet and noticed three things: (1) the model excludes some points in the data set, (2) the model uses some unconventional scheme to calculate an average real GDP growth weight, and (3) a coding error resulted in the exclusion of five countries. Belgium, for instance, was excluded and it has 26 years with debt-to-GDP above 90 percent, with an average growth rate of 2.6 percent. It is not possible to obtain the published results without this error, and it most likely explains why it has been impossible for others to replicate these results.

While adopting a spreadsheet engineering approach does not guarantee an error-free model, it is the best option to create verifiably valid spreadsheets. The following process (suggested by [8]) is based on spreadsheet engineering principles:

1. Before even launching the spreadsheet application, draw a picture to better understand the business situation. Identify the parameters (uncontrollable inputs), the decision variables, and the outputs. Define the logic necessary to transform the inputs into the outputs.
2. Sketch out, on paper, an overall plan for the model. In general, group the inputs together. Determine where the inputs, intermediate calculations, constraints (if any), and outputs will go. Plan to highlight the key inputs and outputs to make the model easier to use by others and for what-if analysis. Determine the formulas relating the inputs to the intermediate calculations and outputs. This can be very simple for some models (e.g., profit = revenue - expenses), or it may be quite complicated, and therefore planning is crucial. In general, the time spent planning a model in this step is normally much less than the time spent debugging an unplanned, completed model.
3. Develop the base case spreadsheet model. Group the inputs together logically. It usually helps to use a color-coding scheme so the user can quickly determine what are the inputs and outputs of the model. Break down the intermediate calculations so that each formula is relatively simple. There is little gain in minimizing the number of cells by using overly complex formulas. Use specific text labels,

---

[1] EuSpRIG Horror Stories can be found at http://www.eusprig.org/horror-stories.htm.

[2] VaR (Value at Risk) is a popular measure of the risk of loss on a specific portfolio of financial assets.

including units of measure, so that others reading the model can follow its logic. The outputs should also be clearly labeled and color-coded. For large models (generally speaking, those that do not fit in a window screen), it is often very helpful to provide a summary of the outputs next to the inputs.

4. Test the spreadsheet model using trial values. Use both "realistic" and "unrealistic" input values in order to detect errors. As we mentioned before, assuming that a spreadsheet model is error-free is not a sensible assumption. Thus, you need to scrutinize formulas and results during and after the spreadsheet development effort. Whenever possible, verify the results by hand. This is easier if, as suggested in the previous step, complex formulas are broken down into intermediate calculations that include relatively simple formulas.
5. Use the model to perform the analysis needed to answer the questions related to the business situation. This may involve producing a relatively simple table, the preparation of a chart, or more substantial analysis. Two common types of analysis are scenario analysis and sensitivity analysis. A scenario is a specific set of conditions that could occur in a real situation. A common practice is to examine the base-case, best-case, and worst-case scenarios. Scenario analysis helps a decision maker gain some insight into the risk related to the decisions that he/she needs to make. Sensitivity analysis involves studying the changes to the output of the model (e.g., profit) as one or more of the inputs (e.g., demand) change. Sensitivity analysis helps to identify the inputs that cause the most change in the output. Since the values for the inputs are often just the best available estimates, it is important to understand which inputs are more critical than others in terms of their effect on the outputs. Break-even analysis is one special case of sensitivity analysis. No matter how simple or complex the analysis, the time invested developing a high-quality base-case model will pay off when you need to do additional analysis. Spreadsheet software includes a number of tools to assist the analyst; we will provide an overview of these in the next section.
6. Document the model so that others can easily understand it. Since others may not think of the problem in exactly the way you do, descriptive labels and a logical layout are extremely important. Indeed, ideal spreadsheet models are almost "self-documented" as a result of the way they are organized and labeled. Cell comments, range names, split windows, are only a few of the formatting options available in most electronic spreadsheet packages that allow the developer to create well-documents and easy to follow models.

Spreadsheet modeling is not a science. However, given the importance of spreadsheet in the decision-making process of many business around the world, following guidelines similar to the ones discussed above is of critical importance when building spreadsheet models. There is evidence indicating that spreadsheet errors are not at all uncommon and that these errors have led to bad decisions and inadequate policies. Proceeding with care and caution when developing spreadsheets is an understated advice.

1.2 Analysis Tools

Analysis is at the core of why spreadsheets are popular models to support decision making. Spreadsheet software packages include a large number of analysis tools (e.g., those related to statistical analysis). Independent vendors provide additional tools for more complex situations (e.g., Crystal Ball by Oracle). In general, however, the following are typical analysis tools in spreadsheet environments:

- Data Analysis
- What-if Analysis
- Optimization
- Simulation and Risk Analysis

In the remainder of this book, we make specific reference to Microsoft Excel, a widely popular spreadsheet platform that will help us illustrate our concepts. We will not only use the common Excel functions but will expand Excel's capabilities with Visual Basic for Applications. In addition, we will discuss some enhanced functionality provided by Add-ins developed by third party vendors and open source groups.

Data analysis in Excel includes all the common statistical analysis tools to perform some basic descriptive analytics on data sets, including analysis of variance, correlation analysis, descriptive statistics, histograms, and hypothesis testing. Also, some basic predictive analytics could be performed with tools such as regression, exponential smoothing, and moving average. We do not provide any specific examples on the use of these tools given that they appear in most modern textbooks on business statistics or quantitative methods.

1.2.1 What-If Analysis

What-if analysis refers to the process of assessing the change in output values as it relates to changes in inputs. The analysis is different for each general class of inputs. If the changes occur in parameter values (i.e., uncontrollable inputs), then the analyst is trying to determine the sensitivity of the model outputs to possible errors (or variation) in the estimation of the parameter values. In other words, the analyst is asking what would happen if the information turns out to be different. Perhaps the parameter values were obtained by making some assumptions and the analyst wants to know what outputs to expect if those assumptions turn out to be false. If the change is in decision variables (controllable inputs), then the analyst might be exploring values that provide the best outcome. Or, he/she might be interested in knowing which input values to avoid because they might result in undesired outcomes.

Excel includes three What-if Analysis Tools: Scenario Manager, Goal Seek, and Data Table. We use the following example to illustrate the Scenario Manager tool.

Example 1.1 A manufacturer produces and markets a product, which it stocks in various warehouses throughout the United States. Two production facilities, one in Portland and the other one in Baltimore, can be operated at either 800 thousand or 1 million units per year, with two different associated fixed costs. The company has four warehouses that distribute the product to retailers. Forecasting models provided the demand scenarios for each location shown in Table 1.1.

Table 1.1 Demand scenarios for Example 1.1

Warehouse	Pessimistic	Most likely	Optimistic
Atlanta	300,000	500,000	590,000
Columbus	250,000	300,000	550,000
Los Angeles	420,000	600,000	650,000
Seattle	300,000	400,000	500,000

The shipping costs per unit and the fixed costs (in thousands) are given in Table 1.2.

Table 1.2 Shipping and fixed costs (in thousands) for Example 1.1

Plant	Warehouse				Fixed cost	
	Atlanta	Columbus	Los Angeles	Seattle	800 K	1 M
Baltimore	$0.35	$0.20	$0.85	$0.75	$1,500	$2,000
Portland	$0.85	$0.60	$0.30	$0.10	$1,200	$2,100

The company uses the Baltimore plant to supply Atlanta and Columbus, while the Portland plant supplies LA and Seattle. Each unit of product is sold for $3. The VP of Operations would like to know the profit associated with the following decisions under the three demand scenarios:

A. Operate both plants at 800 K
B. Operate both plants at 1 M
C. Operate Baltimore at 800 K and Portland at 1 M
D. Operate Baltimore at 1 M and Portland at 800K

Note that capacity and demand do not match under most scenarios. Therefore, the spreadsheet model must consider that when the total demand exceeds the total capacity then only a fraction of the demand at each location is satisfied. Figure 1.2 shows the spreadsheet model with the most likely demand scenario and both plants operating at 800 thousand units per year.

Example 1.1

Price	$3	per unit

Revenue	$4,800
Fixed cost	$2,700
Shipping cost	$411
Profit	$1,689

Shipping costs per unit and fixed costs per plant capacity

Location	Warehouse				Fixed Costs		Capacity	
	Atlanta	Columbus	LA	Seattle	800K	1M	800K	1M
Baltimore	$0.35	$0.20	$0.85	$0.75	$1,500	$2,000	800	1000
Portland	$0.85	$0.60	$0.30	$0.10	$1,200	$2,100	800	1000
Demand	500	300	600	400				

Capacity constraints and shipping schedule

Location	Warehouse				Open Plants		Shipped	Available Capacity
	Atlanta	Columbus	LA	Seattle	800K	1M		
Baltimore	500	300			1	0	800	800
Portland			480	320	1	0	800	800
Received	500	300	480	320				

Fig. 1.2 Spreadsheet model for Example 1.1

Blue cells indicate uncontrollable inputs, which include costs and demand. We consider cost as an uncontrollable input because exact values are typically not known with certainty until the end of the year. Green cells indicate controllable inputs, including price and the capacities at which the plants will operate. For reasons that will become clear later in the chapter, we model the decisions related to plant capacities as binary variables (cells `F20:G21`) and therefore the available capacity in cell `I20` is calculated as `SUMPRODUCT(H12:I12,F20:G20)`, with the formula for cell `I21` employing the corresponding cells in rows 13 and 21. The most complex formula in the model corresponds to the calculation of the number of units shipped to a warehouse, i.e., this formula is used for cells `B20`, `C20`, `D21`, and `E21`. The formula must take into account both the demand in the current scenario and the available capacity. The formula corresponding to `B20` (units shipped from Baltimore to Atlanta) is `B14*MIN(1,I20/SUM(B14:C14))`. When the total demand for Atlanta and Columbus (i.e., `SUM(B14:C14)`) exceeds the total capacity of Baltimore (i.e., `I20`) then only the corresponding fraction of the demand is supplied. If there is sufficient capacity then the demand is satisfied in full and hence the value of 1 in the `MIN()` formula. Note, for instance, that in Fig. 1.2 the total estimated demand for LA and Seattle is 1 million units. However, a decision has been made to operate Portland at 800 thousand units. Therefore, only 80% of the demand of both LA and Seattle can be satisfied, resulting in 480 and 320 thousand units.

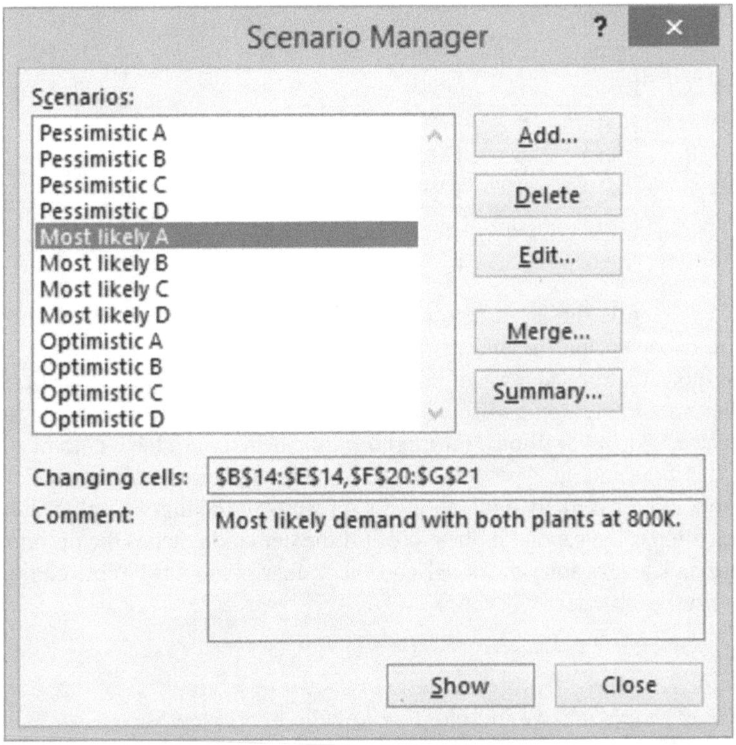

Fig. 1.3 Scenario Manager Window

Once the spreadsheet model has been built and tested, the Scenario Manager tool could be used to manage all the demand scenarios and the decisions that the VP would like to explore. The Scenario Manager tool is in the What-If Analysis drop-down menu of the Data Tools section in the Data tab. For this tool, a scenario is defined as each combination of demand estimate and capacity decisions. Since there are three demand estimates (i.e., pessimistic, most likely, and optimistic) and four capacity decisions (i.e., A, B, C, and D) then there are 12 different scenarios, as shown in Fig. 1.3.

Once all the scenarios have been loaded on the tool, the Summary button produces a table of the output values associated with each scenario. In this case, we select `G3` to `G6` as our output values in order to produce Table 1.3.

Table 1.3 Scenario summary for Example 1.1

Scenario	Revenue	Fixed cost	Shipping cost	Profit
Most likely A	4800	2700	411	1689
Most likely B	5400	4100	455	845
Most likely C	5400	3600	455	1345
Most likely D	4800	3200	411	1189
Optimistic A	4800	2700	393	1707
Optimistic B	6000	4100	491	1409
Optimistic C	5400	3600	435	1365
Optimistic D	5400	3200	448	1752
Pessimistic A	3810	2700	311	799
Pessimistic B	3810	4100	311	–601
Pessimistic C	3810	3600	311	–101
Pessimistic D	3810	3200	311	299

Not surprisingly, the largest profit would be achieved if both plants operate at maximum capacity and the optimistic demand scenario occurs. However, the total profit for this situation ($1.752 million) is only 3.7% higher than the profit obtained under the most likely demand scenario while both plants operate at 800 thousand units per year ($1.689 million). Furthermore, the decision to have both plants operating at 800 thousand units per year seems to be the most robust because both at the pessimistic and most likely demand levels it results in the highest achievable profit. This decision has the second highest profit if the demand reaches the optimistic scenario levels. The spreadsheet model and the scenario summary table can be found in the *Analysis Tools.xlsx* workbook.

Example 1.2 Consider the situation described in Example 1.1. Suppose that the VP of Operations would like to know the breakeven price assuming that the most likely demand scenario will occur and that both plants will be set to operate at 800 thousand units per year. The breakeven price is the one that results in a total profit of zero.

The breakeven price could be found by a simple trial an error process. For instance, we know that the price of $3 results in a profit of $1.689 million under the most likely demand scenario and with both plants operating at 800 thousand units per year (see the row labeled “Most likely A” in Table 1.3). Therefore, the breakeven price must be less than $3 and we could gradually reduce the value until finding one that makes the total profit be almost zero. Alternatively, we can use the Goal Seek tool, which can also be found under the What-If dropdown menu in the Data Tools section of the Data tab. The tool seeks the value of the changing cell (`B3`) that makes the set cell (`G6`) be equal to the desired value (zero). The Goal Seek window is shown in Fig. 1.4.

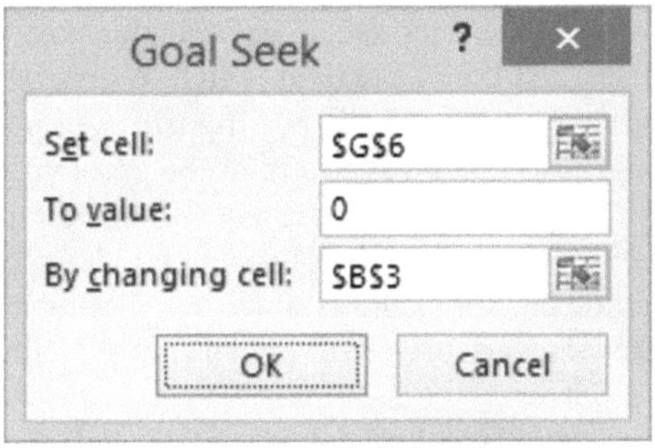

Fig. 1.4 Scenario Manager Window

By clicking OK, we find out that the breakeven price in this situation is $1.94, which results in revenues of $3.111 million, a fixed cost of $2.7 million, and shipping costs of $411 thousand. As mentioned before, for this example it would have been relatively easy to approximate the breakeven price. However, in general, Goal Seek can be a very useful tool for finding the value of an input for a desired value of an output, particularly in situations where the relationship between the input and the output is complex.

1.2.2 Optimization

Optimization is associated with the fundamental managerial question that consists of determining the values of decision variables that achieve the best value of an output. The "best" is a value that is either a minimum (e.g., when the output is cost) or a maximum (e.g., when the output is profit). All the metaheuristic methodologies that we will describe in subsequent chapters enable the solution of optimization models. However, before we move into the world of metaheuristic optimization, we use the following example to illustrate the optimization tool embedded in Excel and known as Solver.

Example 1.3 Suppose that the situation described in Example 1.1 is changed to be one in which the plant locations and their capacities have not be determined. That is, the decision maker has some candidate locations and input data related to these locations have been collected. In particular, let us assume that four locations are being considered (Baltimore, Milwaukee, Portland, and San Antonio) The VP of Operations would like to know where to locate plants to meet the demand of the four warehouses, assuming that the most likely demand scenario will occur.

This problem is known in the Operations Management literature as the plant location problem and can be formulated as a mixed-integer program (MIP). It is a

MIP because it contains both integer decisions variables (i.e., the binary decisions of where to locate plants and the capacity at which to operate them) and continuous variables (i.e., the number of units to be shipped from plants to warehouses). Because of the special transportation structure of the problem, the continuous variables naturally take on integer values without any additional restrictions. Therefore, in the model, these decision variables are not declared to be integer. MIP models are linear in the sense that the equations in the models do not included nonlinear terms associated with the decision variables. MIP models are solved with the Simplex LP solving method within Solver.

Figure 1.5 shows the spreadsheet model associated with this optimization problem. The model is almost identical to the one shown in Fig. 1.2. The only difference is that a Sum column (cells `H22` to `H25`) has been added to the shipping table. This column adds the entries in the Open Plants columns and is used to set up a constraint that restricts operating a plant at only one of the two levels (i.e., either 800 K or 1 M). These decisions determine the available capacity at each location. The values in Fig. 1.5 are the decisions that guarantee an optimal solution, that is, the solution that maximizes the total profit. Note that instead of operating the Baltimore and Portland plants, the optimal solution prescribes to operate the plants in Milwaukee and San Antonio at a production level of 800 thousand units per week. The model has eight binary variables (`F22:G25`) and sixteen continuous variables

	A	B	C	D	E	F	G	H	I
1	Example 1.1								
2									
3	Price	$3	per unit		Revenue		$4,800		
4					Fixed cost		$2,700		
5					Shipping cost		$411		
6					Profit		$1,689		
7									
8	**Shipping costs per unit and fixed costs per plant capacity**								
9									
10	Location	Warehouse				Fixed Costs		Capacity	
11		Atlanta	Columbus	LA	Seattle	800K	1M	800K	1M
12	Baltimore	$0.35	$0.20	$0.85	$0.75	$1,500	$2,000	800	1000
13	Portland	$0.85	$0.60	$0.30	$0.10	$1,200	$2,100	800	1000
14	Demand	500	300	600	400				
15									
16	**Capacity constraints and shipping schedule**								
17									
18	Location	Warehouse				Open Plants		Shipped	Available Capacity
19		Atlanta	Columbus	LA	Seattle	800K	1M		
20	Baltimore	500	300			1	0	800	800
21	Portland			480	320	1	0	800	800
22	Received	500	300	480	320				

Fig. 1.5 Spreadsheet model for Example 1.3

(B22:E25). These variables are continuous because in the optimization model they are not restricted to be integer. However, as mentioned above, the characteristics of the problem are such that these variables will naturally take on integer variables as long as the demand values are integer. The optimal profit is \$2.23 million, which represents an estimated increase of about 32% over the original plan.

The optimal solution shown in the spreadsheet in Fig. 1.5 was found with the Solver tool, which is located in the Analysis section of the Data tab. Figure 1.6 shows the complete optimization model associated with the spreadsheet model in Fig. 1.5.

The objective function in the Solver model shown in Fig. 1.6 states that we want to maximize total profit (G6). It also states that the decision variables (changing variable cells) are both the shipping schedule (B22:F25) and the decisions about which plants to operate and at what level of production (F22:G25). The first set of constraints restricts the sum of the shipments to each location to not exceed the corresponding demand. Because this constraint is not an "equal to" constraint, it does not force to satisfy all the demand. Note that the optimal solution leaves 200 units of demand in Seattle uncovered. It can be easily verified that a solution that covers all the demand is actually suboptimal, forcing San Antonio to operate at the higher production level and resulting in a total profit of \$2.02 million.

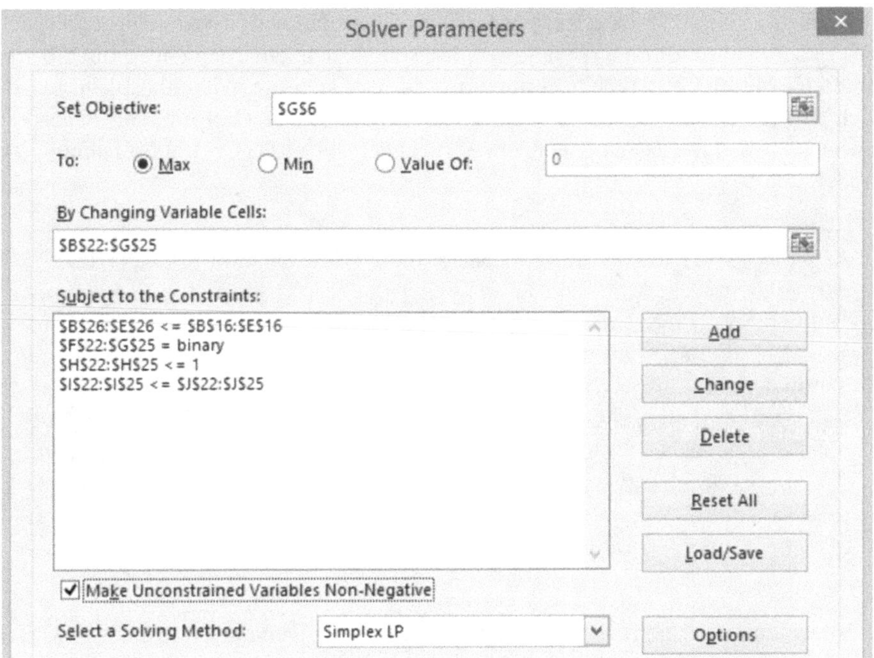

Fig. 1.6 Solver model for Example 1.3

The second constraint in the model of Fig. 1.6 restricts the plant decision variable to be binary. The following constraint limits the production levels in each location to one. That is, it forces the solver to pick no production at all, production of 800 thousand units, or production of 1 million units. The final constraints limits the total shipments from each location to be less than or equal to the available capacity.

1.2.3 Simulation and Risk Analysis

Simulation is a tool that allows us to expand scenario analysis to consider a large number of cases and also assign probability values to them. In Sect. 1.2.1 through scenario analysis, we were able to construct a table that estimates what would happen to key outputs if certain demand scenarios would occur when coupled with production level decisions. The table was constructed assuming three demand levels. Simulation expands this idea by allowing the analyst to make probabilistic assumptions about key data. This means that the analyst can use a probability distribution instead of a point estimate to represent the possible values of a key parameter. In general, simulation is a tool to incorporate uncertainty in decision models. Uncertainty is related to risk and therefore simulation models are considered one the main methods to perform risk analysis.

While it is possible to perform some limited simulation of dynamic process (such as a queuing system) on a spreadsheet, the spreadsheet environment is much better suited for Monte Carlo type of simulations. Several simulation Excel Add-ins exists, such as Oracle's Crystal Ball, Frontline's Analytic Solver Platform, and Palisade's @Risk. We will illustrate the concept of risk analysis with a Crystal Ball simulation model.

Example 1.4 Consider the spreadsheet model developed in Example 1.3. In particular, we are interested in analyzing the risk associated with the optimal solution if the demand is assumed to be uncertain. We use the demand scenarios in Table 1.1 and assume that for each location they represent the parameter values for a triangular distribution of the actual demand. We define four assumptions in a Crystal Ball model, one for each demand value. The binary variables are fixed, with the values shown in Fig. 1.5. For every set of demand values that the simulator produces, a simple transportation problem must be solved. We set up Crystal Ball to use the Solver in each simulation trial, right after generating the demand values.

The solution to the transportation problem for the given demand values produces the optimal revenue and shipping costs and therefore the optimal profit. Since the profit cell (G6) is defined as a Forecast cell, Crystal Ball collects all the profit values generated during the simulation and is capable of calculating a number of statistical measures related to those values. It is also possible to build empirical probability distributions for forecast cells, such as the one shown in Fig. 1.7.

The empirical probability distribution of profit shown in Fig. 1.7 was built by running 1000 trials of the simulation model. It shows that the profit values are concentrated in a fairly narrow range. In particular, the distribution predicts that there is a 90.67% chance that the profit will be between \$2.2 and \$2.3 million. This risk analysis can be taken one step further by combining the simulation model with the optimization of the plant selection and sizing. That is, the analyst could be interested in finding the plant configuration that optimizes some statistical measure associated with the empirical distribution of the profits. For instance, the analysts might want to know what plant configuration maximizes the empirical probability of the total profit reaching more than \$2.250 million. The combination of these two technologies[3] is referred to as simulation-optimization, a topic that we will cover in Chap. 5.

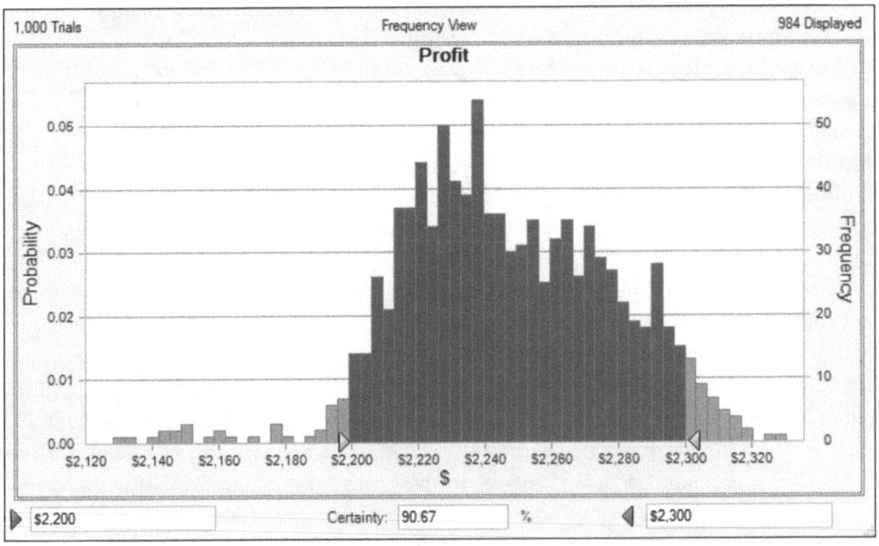

Fig. 1.7 Empirical probability distribution of the profit values in Example 1.4

1.3 Introduction to Metaheuristics

In order to understand what a metaheuristic is, we need to discuss the concept of optimality as it relates to search for a solution in a solution space. An optimization problem consists of finding the best (optimal) feasible solution in a space defined by the solution representation and the problem constraints. A solution is optimal if

[3]This section has been adapted from Sect. 1.1 of the 1997 Tabu Search book by Glover and Laguna.

it minimizes or maximizes the objective function. For instance, in Example 1.3, the objective function is total profit and the optimization problem consists of finding the set of plants and their production capacity that will result in the maximum profit value. The decision problem was mathematically formulated employing a set of eight binary variables in cells `F22` to `G25`. Let us arrange these cells using the following notation:

```
(F22, G22, F23, G23, F24, G24, F25, G25)
```

Then, any solution to the optimization problem can be represented with this binary vector. For instance, the optimal solution shown in Fig. 1.5 can be written as (0,0,1,0,0,0,1,0). Note that there is no need to include the shipping variables (`B22:F25`) in the solution representation because their values are determined by the choices of plant locations and production capacities.

The **solution space** is the set of all possible solutions resulting from a solution representation. The solution space in Example 1.3 consists of all combinations of the binary variables and therefore it has a size of $2^8 = 256$. When the optimization problem includes constraints, the solution space may contain both feasible and infeasible solutions. A **feasible solution** is one that meets all the constraints in the optimization problem. Because of the constraint that limits the production level to be either 800 thousand units or a million units (but not both) in each possible plant location, there are only 81 feasible solutions in the solution space of the Example 1.3 model.

At the core, a metaheuristic is a search methodology that attempts to find the best (optimal) feasible solution in the solution space defined by the solution representation and the set of constraints in the problem. One metaheuristic methodology differentiates from another in the way in which it goes about searching the solution space. We will discuss this in detail in subsequent chapters so at this point it suffices to say that one form of searching consists of transforming one solution into another by a mechanism called **move**. In the binary representation shown above, a typical move entails "flipping" one of the binary variables from its current value to its complementary value, that is, from zero to one or from one to zero.

Now we are ready to define local optimality and illustrate this concept using Example 1.3. A **local optimal** solution in the search space is one for which there is no neighboring solution with a better objective function value, where the neighboring solutions are all those that can be reached in a single move. A **global optimal** solution, on the other hand, is such that no other solution in the search space is better than it. Consider the solution (1,0,0,0,1,0,0,0) that corresponds to Baltimore and Portland both operating at 800 thousand units per year. Assume that a methodology is used to search the solution space by changing a single binary variable from its current value to its complementary value. Then, Table 1.4 shows the 6 neighboring (feasible) solutions along with their corresponding objective function value. The (1,0,0,0,1,0,0,0) solution (first one in the table) is a local optimum because none of its neighboring solutions has a better objective function value. The global optimal solution represented by (0,0,1,0,0,0,1,0) with an objective function value of \$2.23

million is not in the neighborhood of solution (1,0,0,0,1,0,0,0) as defined by the simple flipping move described above. A quest for global optimality requires strategies that will allow the search to go beyond these local optimal solutions, and this is precisely the goal of metaheuristic methodologies.

Table 1.4 Neighboring solutions of the local optimum (1,0,0,0,1,0,0,0)

Solution	Meaning	Obj. Func. Val. (in thousands)
(1,0,0,0,1,0,0,0)	Baltimore (800 K) and Portland (800 K)	\$1,705
(0,0,0,0,1,0,0,0)	Portland (800 K)	\$1,040
(1,0,1,0,1,0,0,0)	Baltimore (800 K), Milwaukee (800 K), and Portland (800 K)	\$1,180
(1,0,0,1,1,0,0,0)	Baltimore (800 K), Milwaukee (1 M), and Portland (800 K)	\$480
(1,0,0,0,0,0,0,0)	Baltimore (800 K)	\$655
(1,0,0,0,1,0,1,0)	Baltimore (800 K), Portland (800 K), and San Antonio (800 K)	\$1,325
(1,0,0,0,1,0,0,1)	Baltimore (800 K), Portland (800 K), and San Antonio (1 M)	\$625

The term meta-heuristic (also written metaheuristic) was coined by Fred Glover in his seminal article "Future Paths for Integer Programming and Links to Artificial Intelligence" [2]. The term has come to be widely applied in the literature. A metaheuristic refers to a methodology that includes master strategies capable of leading the search for the global optimal solution to an optimization problem to areas in the solution space that go beyond those explored by simple heuristics, which tend to focus on finding a single locally optimal solution. The heuristics guided by such a meta-strategy may be high level procedures or may embody nothing more than a description of available moves for transforming one solution into another, together with an associated evaluation rule.

The contrast between the meta-heuristic orientation and the "local optimality" orientation is significant. For many years, the primary conception of a heuristic procedure (a conception that in some ways it is still prevalent today) was to envision either a clever rule of thumb or an iterative rule that terminates as soon as no solutions immediately accessible could improve the last one found. Such iterative heuristics are often referred to as descent methods, ascent methods, or local search methods. Consequently, the emergence of methods that departed from this classical design and that did so by means of an organized master design constituted an important advance. Widespread awareness of this advance only began to dawn during the late 1980s, though its seeds go back much farther.

Metaheuristics in their modern forms are based on a variety of interpretations of what constitutes "intelligent" search. These interpretations lead to design choices that in turn can be used for classification purposes. However, a rigorous classification of different metaheuristics is a difficult and risky enterprise, because the leading advocates of alternative methods often differ among themselves about the essential nature of the methods they espouse. This may be illustrated by considering the classification of metaheuristics in terms of their features with respect to three basic design choices: (1) the use of adaptive memory, (2) the kind of neighborhood exploration used, and (3) the number of current solutions carried from one iteration to the next. These options may be embedded in a classification scheme of the form $x/y/z$, where the choices for x are A (if the meta-heuristic employs adaptive memory) and M (if the method is "memoryless"). The choices for y are N (for a method that employs some systematic neighborhood search either to select the next move or to improve a given solution) and S (for those methods relying on random sampling). Finally, z may be 1 (if the method moves from one current solution to the next after every iteration) or P (for a population-based approach with a population of size P). This simple 3-dimensional scheme gives us a preliminary basis of classification, which discloses that agreement on the proper way to label various metaheuristics is far from uniform. Table 1.5 shows this by providing classifications for the metaheuristics that will be discussed in Chaps. 3–4.

The classifications in Table 1.5 most closely matches the most common implementations of these methodologies. However, they are not the only possibility due to the hybridization that has occurred over the years with many of the strategies that have been suggested. For instance, as we will see in Chap. 3, GRASP relies both in random sampling to construct solutions but also in neighborhood search to try to improve them. The most common implementation of the method does not use memory structures. However, hybrid proposals include memory structures similar to those employed in tabu search. On the other hand, simulated annealing employs a random sampling scheme to choose a solution in the neighborhood of the current solution. Most implementations are memoryless and hence the choice of M in the first dimension of the classification in Table 1.5. However, some variants include a step in which the search returns to the stage (temperature) where the best solution was found. This implies that the stage needs to be store in a memory structure. Variable neighborhood search uses moves of various complexity to search the solution space and for the most part those not rely on random mechanisms with the exception of a shaking step. Finally, tabu search is well-known for its use of adaptive memory

Table 1.5 Metaheuristic classification

Metaheuristic	Classification
GRASP	M/SN/1
Variable neighborhood search	M/N/1
Tabu search	A/N/1

and less reliance in random elements, as discussed in Chap. 4. We point out that in this book we focus on methods that explore the solution space by maintaining a single solution that is transformed during the process. We limit our discussion of population-based procedures to their role in building black-box optimizers, as discussed in Chap. 5.

In addition to the three basic design elements used in the above classification, metaheuristics incorporate other strategies with the goal of guiding the search. Note that all searches eventually reach a local optimum and therefore they need to include rules that will allow them to "escape" local optimality. Consider the situation that we describe above based on Example 1.3 and that we summarize as follows:

Current solution: (1,0,0,0,1,0,0,0)
Objective function value: $1,705
Move mechanism: Change a single variable value (0 to 1 or 1 to 0)
Feasibility rule: Allow only feasible moves (i.e., moves to feasible solutions)

Table 1.4 shows the neighboring feasible solutions of the solution that we are assuming a search procedure is currently visiting. As we stated before, the current solution is also a local optimal solution according to the allowed moves. We can calculate the **move value** as the difference between the objective function value of the neighboring solution and the objective function value of the current solution. Clearly, in this example, all the move values to the neighboring solutions are negative, since the objective function values of the neighboring solutions are all inferior to the one of the current solution. A negative move value in a maximization problem indicates a deterioration of the objective function, when measured against the objective function value of the current solution. If the rules of the search are such that no deterioration of the objective function is allowed (i.e., only improving moves are considered), than the search must terminate at this point. However, if the search terminates now, then the global optimal solution or better local optimal solutions are not found. To deal with this situation, a metaheuristic may strategically modify the move evaluation. For example, a metaheuristic may consider all improving moves equally attractive and any such move encountered is accepted. Deteriorating moves are probabilistically accepted or rejected by initially assigning a high probability to accepting any move generated and gradually reducing the probability of accepting such moves. This simple strategy allows the search to escape local optimal solutions by moving to an inferior neighboring solution and it is the basis for a methodology known as simulated annealing, which we will explore later in the book.

A metaheuristic may also modify the moves considered to be available, by excluding some members and introducing others. This amended neighborhood definition may itself necessitate a change in the nature of the move evaluation. For instance, suppose that at a particular step, a metaheuristic procedure allows the search to move from the (1,0,0,0,1,0,0,0) solution in Table 1.4 to the best feasible neighboring solution, i.e., (1,0,0,0,1,0,1,0) with an objective function value of $1325. Then the unmodified neighborhood of the new current solution (1,0,0,0,1,0,1,0) includes the previous current solution (1,0,0,0,1,0,0,0). However, since the search already visited that solution and the neighborhood of that solution was already explored, a possible metaheuristic strategy could consist of forbidding the search to move back to that previous solution. This means that the neighborhood of the current solution has been modified by forbidding a move and therefore excluding a member of the original neighborhood. This is the basis of a metaheuristic methodology known as tabu search and whose details will be provided in a later chapter.

Consider also the methodology known as strategic oscillation that was suggested a number of years ago in connection with tabu search. It illustrates the intimate relationship between changes in neighborhood and changes in evaluation. A standard neighborhood, like the one in Table 1.4, that allows moves only among feasible solutions might be enlarged by the strategic oscillation approach to include infeasible solutions. The search is then strategically driven to cross the feasibility boundary to proceed into the infeasible region. After a selected depth is reached, the search changes direction to drive back toward feasibility, and upon crossing the feasibility boundary similarly continues in the direction of increased feasibility. (One-sided oscillations are employed in some variants to remain predominantly on a particular side of the boundary.) To guide these trajectories, the approach modifies customary evaluations to take account of the induced direction of movement and the region in which the movement occurs. The result generates a controlled behavior that exploits the theme of non-monotonic exploration.

In the way that the optimization model of our plant-location example (Example 1.3) was formulated the infeasible solutions are those for which more than one plant size is chosen in the same location. Therefore a solution such as (1,1,0,0,1,0,0,0) that prescribed to operate Baltimore at both 800 K and 1 M along with Portland at 800 K is infeasible. There are many situations where the solution space includes both feasible and infeasible solutions, creating a feasibility boundary between the two sets. Crossing that boundary from both sides of the search space has been shown to be an effective way of finding good solutions and hence the increasing popularity of the strategic oscillation approach. The effectiveness of this approach is related to the high frequency by which the best solutions tend to be close to the feasibility boundary. In linear programming models, for instance, optimal solutions resided precisely on the feasibility boundary.

The emphasis on guidance differentiates a metaheuristic from a simple random restart procedure or a random perturbation procedure. A random restart process in our example would be one for which an initial solution is found by randomly setting some of the binary variables to 1. Likewise, a random perturbation would such that given a solution, a variable is randomly selected and its value is “flipped” from zero to one or from one to zero. However, sometimes these naive restarting and perturbation procedures are also classed as low-level metaheuristics, since they allow an opportunity to find solutions that are better than a first local optimum encountered. “Noising” procedures, which introduce controlled randomized changes in parameters such as cost or resource availability coefficients, provide one of the popular mechanisms for implementing such approaches. Another popular mechanism is simply to randomly modify evaluations, or to choose randomly from evaluations that fall within a chosen window. Such randomized processes are also applied to selecting different types of moves (neighborhood definitions) at different junctures. The greedy randomized adaptive search procedure (GRASP), described in a subsequent chapter, is based on this controlled-randomized schemes.

The original conception of a metaheuristic does not exclude consideration of constructive or destructive moves for generating initial solutions, but likewise allows these moves to be subjected to metaheuristic guidance. In other words, metaheuristics are not only used in connection with "transition" moves, which operate on fully constructed solutions. From a broader perspective, a partial solution created by a constructive process is simply viewed as a solution of a particular type, and procedures for generating such solutions are natural candidates to be submitted to higher level guidance. This view has significant consequences for the range of strategies available to a metaheuristic approach, and it is the basis of both strategic oscillation and GRASP. In strategic oscillation, constructive moves are complemented by creating associated destructive moves, allowing the oscillation to proceed constructively to (and beyond) a stipulated boundary, and then to reverse direction to proceed destructively to various depths, in alternating waves. Transition moves permit refinements at varying levels of construction and destruction. In GRASP, constructive or destructive moves are used to create an initial solution that is then subjected to an improvement process. The early perspective that restricted attention only to transition moves gradually eroded, as researchers recognized that such a restriction inhibited the development of effective methods.

1.3.1 Adaptive Memory and Population-Based Strategies

The metaheuristic classification in Table 1.5, which differentiates between population-based strategies and adaptive memory strategies, is often taken to be a fundamental distinction in the literature. Population-based strategies manipulate a collection of solutions rather than a single solution at each stage. Such procedures are typically referred to as composing the class of evolutionary methods. A prominent subclass of these methods is based on strategies for "combining" solutions, as illustrated by genetic algorithms, scatter search and path relinking methods. Another prominent subclass consists of methods that are primarily driven by utilizing multiple heuristics to generate new population members. This incorporation of multiple heuristics for generating trial solutions, as opposed to relying on a single rule or decision criterion, is a very old strategy whose origins are probably not traceable. The key to differentiating the contributions of such methods obviously rests on the novelty of the component heuristics and the ingenuity of the strategies for coordinating them. Such concerns are more generally the focus of parallel processing solution methods, and many "evolutionary" contributions turn out chiefly to be a subset of the strategies that are being developed to a higher level of sophistication under the parallel processing rubric.

The adaptive memory classification provides a more precise means of differentiation, although it is not without pitfalls. From a naive standpoint, virtually all heuristics other than complete randomization induce a pattern whose present state depends on the sequence of past states, and therefore incorporate an implicit form of "memory." Given that the present is inherited from the past, the accumulation of previous choices is in a loose sense "remembered" by current choices. This sense is slightly more pronounced in the case of solution combination methods such as genetic algorithms and scatter search, where the mode of combination more clearly lends itself to transmitting features of selected past solutions to current solutions. Such an implicit memory, however, does not take a form normally viewed to be a hallmark of an intelligent memory structure. In particular, it uses no conscious design for recording the past and no purposeful manner of comparing previous states or transactions to those currently contemplated. By contrast, at an opposite end of the spectrum, procedures such as branch and bound and A* search use highly (and rigidly) structured forms of memory forms that are organized to generate all nondominated solution alternatives with little or no duplication. This is why rigid procedures such as branch-and-bound, when run to completion, are able to identify and verify global optimal solutions. Metaheuristic methods, even those that explicitly employ adaptive memory strategies, search for global optimal solution and frequently find them but cannot verify them. Incidentally, branch and bound is the method behind the Simplex LP engine (see Fig. 1.6) that we chose to solve the MIP model of Example 1.3. Hence, the solution shown in Fig. 1.5 has been verified to be a global optimum.

Adaptive memory procedures, properly conceived, embody a use of memory that falls between these extremes, based on the goal of combining flexibility and ingenuity. Such methods typically seek to exploit history in a manner inspired by (but not limited to) human problem solving approaches. They are primarily represented by tabu search and its variations that sometimes receive the "adaptive memory programming" label. Other non-tabu search approaches have undertaken to incorporate various aspects of such memory structures and strategies, typically in rudimentary form. Developments that produce hybrids of tabu search with other approaches at a more advanced level have become an important avenue for injecting adaptive memory into other methods, and constitute an active area of research.

Another distinction based on memory is introduced by neural network (NN) approaches. Such methods emphasize an associative form of memory, which has its primary application in prediction and pattern matching problems. Neural network procedures also implicitly involve a form of optimization and have been adapted to several optimization settings, although their primary application continues to be predictive analytics. Performance in optimization has been somewhat mixed, but researchers often regard neural networks as appropriate to be included within the metaheuristic classification. Such an inclusion is reinforced by the fact that NN-based optimization approaches sometimes draw on standard heuristics, and produce solutions by transformations that are not limited to ordinary notions of local optimality. A number of initiatives have successfully combined neural networks with simulated annealing, genetic algorithms, and tabu search.

Metaheuristics are often viewed as composed of processes that are intelligent, but in some instances the intelligence belongs more to the underlying design than to the particular character (or behavior) of the method itself. The distinction between intelligent design and intelligent behavior can be illustrated by considering methods that exploit ingenious insights to solve a particular classes of problems. These methods are often remarkably effective for achieving the purposes for which they were devised. Yet it seems doubtful whether such methods should be labeled as intelligent, in the sense of being highly responsive to varying conditions, or of changing the basis for their decisions over time as a function of multiple considerations. It must be conceded that the line that demarcates intelligent methods from other methods is not entirely precise. For this reason it is not necessary for a master procedure to qualify as intelligent in a highly rigorous sense in order to be granted membership in the category of metaheuristics.

1.3.2 Metaphors of Nature

A popular thrust of many research initiatives, and especially of publications designed to catch the public eye, is to associate various methods with processes found in nature. This trend embodies a wave of "New Romanticism," reminiscent of the Romanticism of the 18th and 19th centuries (distinguished by their preoccupation with Nature with a capital "N"). The fascination with natural phenomena as a foundation for problem-solving methods undoubtedly is fueled by our sense of mystery concerning the ability of such phenomena to generate outcomes that are still far beyond our comprehension. However, the New Romanticism goes farther, to suggest that by mimicking the rules we imagine to operate in nature (especially "rudimentary" processes of nature) we will similarly be able to produce remarkable outcomes.

Models of nature that are relied upon for such inspiration are ubiquitous, and it is easy to conjure up examples whose metaphorical possibilities have not yet been tapped. In 1997, Glover and Laguna [3] sarcastically stated:

> To take an excursion in the lighter side of such possibilities (though not too far from the lanes currently traveled), we may observe that a beehive offers a notable example of a system that possesses problem solving abilities. Bees produce hives of exceptional quality and complexity, coordinate diverse tasks among different types of individuals, perform spatial navigation, and communicate via multiple media. (It is perhaps surprising in retrospect that the behavior of bees has not been selected as a basis for one of the 'new' problem solving methods.)

Eight years later, in 2005, the Bees Algorithm was proposed. The main issue with metaheuristics based on metaphors of nature is not that finding inspiration in such processes is inherently bad. The problem is that metaphors are cheap and easy to come by and they are often used to "window dress" a method. Nowadays, these so-called "novel" methods employ analogies that range from intelligent water drops, musicians playing jazz, imperialist societies, leapfrogs, kangaroos, all types of swarms and insects and even mine blast processes. In the serious metaheuristic literature, researchers that use metaphors to stimulate their own ideas about new methods must translate these ideas into metaphor-free language, so that the strategies employed can be clearly understood, and their novelty is made clearly visible.

These analogies to systems in nature invite us to ponder a key question. If we were allowed to place our bets on the probable success of a hive of bees or an anthill, as opposed to that of a group of humans, when confronted with a challenging task that requires intelligence and the ability to learn from the past, how would we wager? Undoubtedly we would be drawn to reflect that our goals and problem structures may often be different than those to which "natural processes" apply. In addition, we ourselves - as products of a rather special and extended chain of natural developments - may incorporate capabilities not present in the processes that produced us.

Some metaphors of nature have had a place. For example, metaphors spurred ideas to launch the first phases of investigations that produced genetic algorithms and the simulated annealing methodology. Fortunately, care was taken to prevent those metaphors from cutting off lines of inquiry beyond their scope. For instance, local searches were added to the original genetic algorithms even though this strategy did not have an immediate interpretation in terms of the process of evolution. Unfortunately, in many cases, metaphors are not a source of inspiration and they seem to be limited to providing a means for "dressing up" the descriptions of various metaheuristic proposals in a way that appeals to our instinct to draw parallels between simple phenomena and abstract designs. Within the realm of metaheuristic design, there is a great deal we have yet to learn. The issue of whether the analogies that underlie some of our models may limit or enhance our access to further discovery deserves careful reflection and requires a component-based view of heuristic search [9].

In this view, new proposals must be adequately framed in the existing literature by deconstructing them and describing their components, measuring their contribution, and making connections to other procedures where similar components appear. To advance the field, clear explanation must be provided on how components are adapted to solve specific problems. Implementation of metaheuristic methods should be explained by employing standard optimization terminology, where, for instance, a solution is called a solution and not something else related to a metaphor.

References

1. Evans, J.R. 2013. *Business analytics*. London: Pearson.
2. Glover, F. 1986. Future paths for integer programming and links to artificial intelligence. *Computers and Operations Research* 13:533–549.
3. Glover, F., and M. Laguna. 1997. Tabu search. Berlin: Springer.
4. Grossman, T.A. 2002. Spreadsheet engineering: A research framework. In *Proceedings of the European spreadsheet risks interest group symposium*. Cardiff, Wales.

5. Grossman, T.A. 2006. Integrating spreadsheet engineering in a management science course: A hierarchical approach. *INFORMS Transactions on Education* 7(1): 18–36.
6. Powell, S.G., and K.R. Baker. 2004. The art of modeling with spreadsheets: Management science, spreadsheet engineering, and modeling craft. New York: Wiley, Inc.
7. Ragsdale, Cliff T. 2014. *Spreadsheet modeling and decision analysis: A practical introduction to business analytics*, 7th ed. Boston: Cengage Learning.
8. Reid, R.D., and N.R. Sanders. 2012. *Operations management*, 5th edn. New York: Wiley.
9. Sörensen, K. 2013. Metaheuristics the metaphor exposed. *International Transactions in Operational Research* 22: 3–18.

Chapter 2
General Concepts in Metaheuristic Search

Metaheuristics have become a very popular family of solution methods for optimization problems because they are capable of finding "acceptable" solutions in a "reasonable" amount of time. Most optimization problems in practice are too complex to be approached by exact methods that can guarantee finding global optimal solutions. The time required to find and verify globally optimal solutions is impractical in most applications. An entire computational theory, which we will not discussed here, has been developed around problem complexity. It suffices to say that it is now known that the great majority of the optimization problems found in practice fall within a category that makes them "computationally intractable." Having accepted the reality that solution methods that yield verifiable globally optimal solutions are not practical, we must apply criteria derived from the problem context to determine what is an acceptable solution and what is reasonable amount of time. For instance, some timetabling problems (e.g., scheduling of courses at University) are notoriously difficult because they include many constraints. Therefore, an acceptable solution in this context could be one that violates the least number of constraints or one that improves a collective preference function value by a relatively small percentage over a solution found by a human scheduler. Comparisons against "manual" solutions are popular in practical problems and help define what is acceptable. Knowledge of the problem context is also necessary to define what is reasonable in terms of solution time. The range is wide. For instance, if an optimization problem is being solved to help a company make strategic decisions then reasonable solution times might be measured in weeks, or even months. These decisions are long range and involve budgets that are in the millions or billions of dollars. On the other end of the spectrum, there are optimization problems that need to be solved in "real time". For example, pricing problems in revenue management systems such as those used by airlines often need to be solved instantaneously in order to update airfares as demand changes. In fact, there are systems that uniquely identify and evaluate each passenger request to determine the optimal price based on revenue management and business strategies.

A. Duarte et al., *Metaheuristics for Business Analytics*, EURO Advanced Tutorials on Operational Research, https://doi.org/10.1007/978-3-319-68119-1_2

The choice of the metaheuristic to use is related to the solution time. It is well-known that, given enough solution time, well-conceived implementations of any metaheuristic methodology tend to perform at about the same level. That is, if competing well-conceived implementations are executed for an inordinate amount of time, it is very likely that the differences in the solutions that they find are not statistically significant. However, given that the strategies vary from one methodology to another, their performance profile also varies. The performance profile is a plot of the value of the objective function associated with the best solution found during the search against the solution time.

As stated by Laguna et al. [3], every metaheuristic procedure is built by considering that to be effective it must include strategies for both search diversification and intensification (also known as exploration and exploitation, respectively). Intensification refers to mechanisms and parameter settings that encourage the addition of solution features that historically (i.e., during the search) have been found to have merit. It also refers to strategies that focus the search on a particular region of attraction. These strategies must be balanced with diversification processes that expand the exploration of the solution space. The opportunity for search diversification depends on the "optimization horizon", that is the length of the optimization process (typically limited by a number of algorithmic iterations, total computational time, or number of objective function evaluations). The optimization horizon relates to the "reasonable" amount of time discussed above and therefore is associated with the problem context. The merit of exact optimization approaches that are expected to run to completion (i.e., that are configured to find and confirm optimal solutions) is measured exclusively by running time. In the realm of metaheuristics, merit is measured with a combination of the quality of the best solution found and the associated computational time to find it. Consider, for instance, the performance profile (i.e., the objective function value of the best solution found during the search) of two hypothetical metaheuristic procedures applied to a minimization problem (see Fig. 2.1).

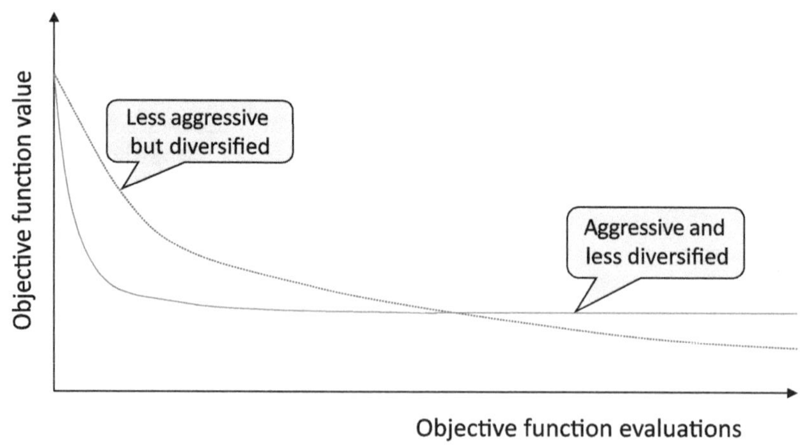

Fig. 2.1 Performance profiles of two hypothetical metaheuristic procedures

As depicted in Fig. 2.1, the search strategies and the parameter values of a particular procedure may be set to perform a search that initially is less aggressive (with respect to an early intensification process) but that, given enough computational time, it is able to steadily find improved outcomes (see dashed line). On the other hand, a procedure may intensify early in the search but may lack diversification strategies that would allow it to improve upon the incumbent solution later in the search. Ideally, a procedure should be able to do both, intensify and diversify in order to meet the goals of the analyst. Clearly, the best choice of metaheuristic design and the associated values of the search parameters to trigger intensification and diversification stages depend on the optimization horizon. In Fig. 2.1, the "Aggressive and less Diversified" procedure represented by the solid line is preferable for a short optimization horizon while the "Less Aggressive but Diversified" represented by the dashed line would be preferable in a problem context where the optimization horizon is relatively long.

The way metaheuristic methods balance search intensification and diversification varies. There are two main distinctions in the classification presented in Table 1.5: population-based procedures versus single-solution based procedures and the use of randomization. In general, population-based procedures maintain diversification by measuring dissimilarities among the solutions in the population. It is then said that a population "converges" when the solutions in the population become "too similar" to each other. If the similarity measure reaches a predetermined threshold, a mechanism is triggered to avoid what is called "premature convergence." This concept refers to a situation where the population has no diversity too early in the optimization horizon. The mechanisms that could be triggered to avoid premature convergence often include some form of randomization. That is, some totally random or semi-random solutions are added to a population in order to induce diversity. Other strategies include the use of memory, where solutions are constructed in such a way that are not only different from those in the current population but also avoid attributes that have been present in solution already explored during the search.

In this book, we focus on single-solution based metaheuristics. In these methodologies, intensification strategies are based on applying a local search to a diverse solution, modifying choice rules to encourage move combinations and solution features historically found to produce high quality solutions, or applying a variety of neighborhood structures. They may also initiate a return to attractive regions to search them more thoroughly. Attractive regions are associated with the concept of elite solutions. Membership in the elite set is often determined by setting a threshold that is connected to the objective function value of the best solution found during the search. Elite solutions can either be used to trigger intensification phases designed to examine their immediate neighborhoods or to expand the neighborhood of another solution. Hence, the main difference between intensification and diversification is that during an intensification stage the search focuses on examining neighborhoods while diversification focuses on moving the search to regions of the solution space that have largely remained unexplored.

During intensification stages, the term “neighbor” may have a broader meaning than in the usual context of neighborhood search. That is, in addition to considering solutions that are adjacent or close to the current solution by means of standard move mechanisms (e.g., flipping the values of a single binary variable as shown in Table 1.4), intensification strategies may generate neighbors by either grafting together components of elite solutions or by using modified evaluations that favor the introduction of such components. The diversification stage on the other hand encourages the search process to examine unvisited regions and to generate solutions that differ in various significant ways from those seen before. Again, such an approach can be based on generating subassemblies of solution components that are then “fleshed out” to produce full solutions, or can rely on modified evaluations as embodied, for example, in the use of penalty/incentive functions designed to discourage/encourage the addition of certain solution features.

2.1 Solution Representation

How to represent a solution is a fundamental design question in metaheuristic optimization. The solution representation is the main factor that determines the form and size of the search space. Therefore, the efficiency of the search is very much dependent on the choice of the solution representation. The representation also determines how the objective function will be evaluated and how the move mechanisms (also referred to as search operators) will create neighborhoods. Consider the following example adapted from [4].

Example 2.1 A pharmaceutical company is hiring five new salespeople to expand its sales in a western state. Pharmaceutical sales representatives do not sell directly to doctors because doctors do not purchase and distribute drugs. However, doctors do write prescriptions, and it is that activity the sales representatives try to influence. The pharmaceutical company is focusing its efforts on the 10 counties in the state and estimated the number of doctors in each county as shown in the last column of Table 2.1. This table also shows ten possible sales regions (comprising contiguous sets of counties) that the company has identified.

For instance, if a sales representative is assigned to region 1, he or she would be responsible for counties 1, 3, and 5. Each sales representative may be assigned to only a single sales region, so only half of the sales regions will be used. The company would like to assign the five sales representatives to the possible regions in such a way that at least one sales representative covers each county. If a county is covered by more than one sales representative, the doctors in the county are split equally among the sales representatives covering the county. The company is concerned about fairness and therefore would like to find the set of regions that will result in a total number of doctors assigned to each sales representative be as equal as possible.

Table 2.1 Number of doctors per county and definition of sales region for Example 2.1

County	Sales region										Doctors
	1	2	3	4	5	6	7	8	9	10	
1	1		1		1						113
2		1		1		1		1			106
3	1		1				1			1	84
4		1		1							52
5	1				1			1			155
6		1				1				1	103
7			1				1		1		87
8		1			1			1			91
9				1			1		1		128
10			1			1				1	131

Solutions to selection problems such as the one described in Example 2.1 are typically represented with binary variables. In this case, we can define 10 binary variables, one for each region, where a value of one represents that the corresponding region has been selected and a value of zero represents that the region has not been selected. That is, the solution is represented by a binary vector of size 10. For instance, the selection of regions 1, 3, 4, 8, and 9 is represented as follows:

$$(1,0,1,1,0,0,0,1,1,0)$$

The search space is then defined by all binary vectors of size 10. This means that the space consists of $2^{10} = 1,024$ solutions. However, not all of these solutions are feasible. Note that there are only 5 sales representatives and the selection must be such that all counties are covered. Therefore only those solutions (binary vectors) that include exactly 5 ones and 5 zeros are possible and within those only the ones that cover all counties are feasible. The number of possible region selections can be calculated as the total number of ways for choosing 5 regions out of 10:

$$\binom{10}{5} = \frac{10!}{5!(10-5)!} = 252$$

A complete examination of all these region selections reveals that only 114 are feasible. The remaining 138 selections fail to cover all the counties. The binary solution representation creates a search space for which only approximately 11% of the solutions are feasible. In other words, the solution space is a relatively small fraction of the search space, when considering searches that are allowed to traverse both feasible and infeasible parts of the space.

Consider an alternative (discrete value) representation consisting of the identities of the selected regions. A solution is then represented by five discrete values in the range from 1 to 10. Therefore, the selection of regions 1, 3, 4, 8, and 9 is represented as follows:

$$(1, 3, 4, 8, 9)$$

This representation creates a search space with a size of $10^5 = 100,000$ solutions. The search space is much larger because it includes both infeasible solutions (i.e., all those for which a region is selected more than once and/or the selected regions do not cover all the counties) and duplicate solutions (i.e., solutions that only differ in the order in which the selected regions appear in the solution). This space can be significantly reduced by imposing a constraint requiring the selected regions to be all different. This all different constraint reduces the space to $10 \times 9 \times 8 \times 7 \times 6 = 30,240$ solutions. The space is still larger than the one induced by the binary representation because of all the duplicates. Note that, without imposing any other restriction, the solution representation allows for 120 (i.e., 5!) ways to represent the selection of the same set of regions. For instance, $(1, 3, 4, 8, 9)$ is the same as (8, 3, 9, 1, 4), and it is also the same as any other permutation of the same numbers. If we divide 30,240 by 120, we reduce the size to 252, which is the same space defined by the binary representation.

The choice of a solution representation is guided by the notions of inclusion, connectivity, and efficiency. **Inclusion** refers to whether or not the resulting solution space includes all the feasible solutions to the original problem. In some cases, a solution representation may exclude (intentionally or unintentionally) some feasible solutions. This could simplify the search but may result in excluding some high quality solutions (including the global optimum). Indirect solution representations, described below, have the property of creating more manageable search spaces by sacrificing complete inclusion. **Connectivity** refers to whether or not there exists at least one path of moves that will connect all pairs of solutions in the solution space. For instance, if the representation is a binary vector and the move mechanism to explore the solution space consists of flipping the value of a single variable then it can be shown that all pairs of solutions are connected. In other words, any solution can be transformed into any other one by changing one value at a time. The length of the connecting path between the two solutions is equal to the number of variables that have different values and is called the Hamming distance. Search strategies may affect connectivity, for instance, when a search is not allowed to visit infeasible solutions. Finally, **efficiency** refers to the ease of transformation to move from one solution to another, the size of the induced search space, and the ease of evaluation of the objective function. A solution representation must be chosen in agreement with the move mechanisms that will be used to search the resulting space. In general, efficient representations are able to absorb some of the problem complexities. For instance, in Example 2.1, the binary representation does not limit the number of selected regions to five. This means that a separate mechanism needs to be included in the search to distinguish between feasible and infeasible solutions. The discrete-value representation, on the other hand, implicitly enforces the constraint that limits the number of sales representatives to five. However, it results in a much larger solution space where only 0.25% of the solutions are unique and feasible.

Permutation vectors are popular solution representations in a variety of combinatorial optimization problems, including those related to job scheduling and vehicle routing. Consider the following example also adapted from [4].

Example 2.2 A printing shop must schedule ten jobs on a single machine. The processing times and due dates for each job are shown in Table 2.2. The jobs can be performed one after the other and there is no setup time involved. If jobs 1, 2, and 3 were scheduled first in that order, then job 1 would finish in 10 days, job 2 in 21 days, and job 3 in 28 days. Since the due dates for these jobs are 12, 35, and 20, respectively, only job 3 would be late (by 8 days) if the print shop were to use this sequence.

Table 2.2 Processing times and due dates for ten printing jobs

Job	Processing time (days)	Due date
1	10	12
2	11	35
3	7	20
4	5	27
5	3	23
6	7	36
7	5	40
8	5	40
9	12	55
10	11	47

A permutation is a natural and direct solution representation in this sequencing problem. A permutation creates a search space of $10! = 3,628,800$ solutions. In this case, the search space has a one-to-one mapping with the solution space. That is, the search space consists of all feasible solutions to the problem and it does not contain any duplicates.

Permutations are also used as indirect solution representations. For instance, suppose that instead of a single machine, the print shop in Example 2.1 would like to schedule the 10 jobs on two machines. A direct solution representation would need to account for the machine where jobs are assigned in addition to the order in which the jobs will be processed. Instead of using a complex solution representation to account for these two pieces of information, a permutation could be employed as an indirect solution representation. Indirect representation require a mapping function or process to transform the representation into a solution to the problem. A simple transformation in the context of this assignment/sequencing problem may be to "assign the next job in the solution representation to the machine that becomes available first." Let us illustrate this rule to transform a permutation into a solution to the 2-machine problem.

Example 2.3 Suppose that a solution to the two-machine version of the problem described in Example 2.2 is given by (1, 3, 5, 4, 2, 6, 7, 10, 9, 8). Then, job 1 is arbitrarily assigned to machine 1 to start immediately. Job 3, is then assigned to machine 2, because this machine is available now and machine 1 will be available on day 10, after completing job 1. Machine 2 will be available first because job 3 requires 7 days. Therefore job 5 is assigned to machine 2. Job 4 is next in the sequence and it can be assigned to either machine because they both complete their current assignment on day 10. Suppose that machine 1 is arbitrarily selected and the process continues. At the end of the transformation process, the sequences are (1, 4, 6, 10, 8) and (3, 5, 2, 7, 9), for machines 1 and 2, respectively. Figure 2.2 shows a Gantt chart of this solution. In this case, the permutation results in a solution for which both machines are assigned the same number of jobs and both complete all the assigned jobs at the same time on day 38.

Fig. 2.2 Gantt chart of a 2-machine solution

An indirect solution representation is also referred to as encoding in some metaheuristic literature. The processes of transforming the representation into a solution of the problem is then referred to as decoding. In this nomenclature, the transformation rules are the decoder. The encoding in Example 2.3 is the ordering of the jobs (i.e., a permutation vector). The decoder is the assignment of the job to the first machine that becomes available. Implicit in this decoder is the notion that no job will wait for a machine to be available. Depending on the form of the objective function value, this transformation has the potential of excluding high quality solutions. For instance, in some settings, schedulers are as concerned with jobs being late as they are of jobs being early. Tardy jobs may cause customer dissatisfaction, but early jobs incur in inventory cost, may become obsolete, and customers do not pay for them until past the deadline. This just-in-time philosophy translates in what is known in the scheduling literature as nonregular objective functions, because they are not always increasing with the completion time of each job. High quality solutions to a scheduling problem with a nonregular objective function may include idle times. Therefore, a decoder such as the one applied to Example 2.3 is likely to leave out of consideration a number of good solutions and limit the search to only those solutions that do not include idle times. The solutions with no idle time have low total tardiness cost but potentially large total earliness cost.

2.2 Objective Function

In an optimization problem, the objective function is the mathematical representation of the goal to achieve. The goal is stated as a minimization or a maximization of the objective function. The function associates a real value to each of the solutions in the solution space. This value indicates the quality of the solution. Clearly, larger values are associated with the best solution in a maximization problem and smaller values are an indication of higher solution quality in a minimization problem. The objective function plays an important role in guiding a metaheuristic search. When an indirect solution representation is used, the solution representation (encoding) must be transformed (decoded) into a solution of the problem in order to be evaluated by the objective function.

In many problems the objective function is relatively easy to formulate and its properties are such that it can be readily use to measure solution quality and serve as the main guide during the metaheuristic search process. In Example 2.1, the pharmaceutical company has the goal of selecting regions in order to be fair to all of its sales representatives. The company defines fairness as the uniform distribution of the total number of doctors among the sales representatives. More than one objective function may achieve this goal. Here are two possibilities for formulating an objective function to achieve the companys goal:

1. The variance of the number of doctors in each of the selected regions.
2. The difference between the maximum and the minimum number of doctors in the selected regions.

Both objective functions measure the dispersion of the number of doctors corresponding to the regions selected by a particular solution. Minimizing either one of these objective functions will guide an optimization process toward solutions that achieve the companys goal.

Regular objective functions associated with the sequencing problem in Example 2.2 are:

1. Number of tardy jobs.
2. Total number of days by which jobs are tardy.
3. Maximum number of days by which any job is tardy.

All these objective functions are to be minimized to meet customer satisfaction goals. The first one implies that clients would be equally dissatisfied if a job is late by one day or by multiple days. Using this objective function means that the print shop wants to minimize the number of dissatisfied clients. The second objective function assigns a "penalty" to each day that any job is tardy. So, the function attempts to minimize a total penalty. This function could be made client specific by adding a "tardiness penalty" to each job. Then the objective function would attempt to minimize the total weighted tardiness. The third objective function has a flavor of fairness. It attempts to minimize the worst case, i.e., the job that will be the tardiest. High quality solutions obtained with this objective function will tend to all jobs having about the same tardiness. A nonregular objective function could be formulated as an extension of the second objective function above by adding the total number of days by which jobs are early.

To analyze the effect that the objective function has on the search for an optimal solution, let us consider a reduced version of the scheduling problem in Example 2.2. Assume that instead of 10 jobs, the print shop has to schedule only the first 5 jobs. The search space defined by all permutations of these 5 jobs has a size of 120 solutions. We enumerate all these solutions and calculate the three regular objective function values and the nonregular objective function value described above. Table 2.3 shows the value of the optimal solution and the number of optimal solutions in the search space corresponding to each of the objective functions.

Table 2.3 shows that the first and the fourth objective functions are in the opposite end of the spectrum. That is, the solution space includes a fair number (17) of solutions that are optimal with respect to the number of tardy jobs. However, there is only one solution in the space that achieves the optimal value with respect to the total earliness and tardiness. In terms of metaheuristic search, it can be argued that it would be "easier" to find a solution that is optimal with respect to the first objective. Regarding the second and third objective functions, it can be conjectured that they both define equivalent objective value landscapes.

Table 2.3 Characteristics of optimal solutions for four objective functions

Objective Function	Optimal value	Number of optimal solutions
Number of tardy jobs	1	17
Maximum tardiness	1	3
Total tardiness	1	2
Total earliness and tardiness	11	1

The notion of objective function landscapes is important from the point of view of effectiveness of a metaheuristic search, as illustrated by the following example.

Example 2.4 Consider an optimization problem defined on a graph consisting of 6 nodes and 9 edges, as shown in Fig. 2.3. The numbers next to an edge represent a dissimilarity measure between the objects at each end of the edge. For instance, the dissimilarity between node A and node B is 6. The problem consists of selecting 3 nodes that are dissimilar. Two objective functions being considered are:

1. The sum of the dissimilarities between all the selected nodes.
2. The minimum node dissimilarity, where the dissimilarity of a node is calculated as the sum of the dissimilarities between itself and all the other selected nodes connected to it.

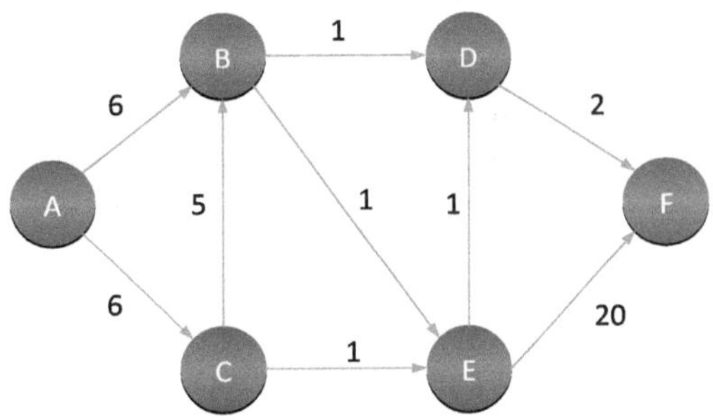

Fig. 2.3 Graph for Example 2.4

The first objective function is very common for these types of problems and it refers to a measure of dispersion efficiency. The second objective function is related to a class of problems for which equity is important and hence these problems belong to what is known as equitable dispersion. A solution to this problem can be represented as a discrete-value vector of size three, indicating the nodes that have been selected. For instance, the solution (A, B, C) represents the selections of nodes A, B, and C. The value of the first objective function (i.e., the sum of all the dissimilarities) is $6 + 5 + 6 = 17$. The value of the second objective function (i.e., the minimum node dissimilarity) is 11 because the dissimilarity of node A is $6 + 6 = 12$ and the dissimilarities of nodes B and C are $6 + 5 = 11$. These two objective functions create a significantly different objective function landscape, as shown in Figs. 2.4 and 2.5.

To create Fig. 2.4, we evaluated all 20 solutions to the problem employing the objective function that aggregates all the dissimilarities of the selected nodes. (Note that there are 20 unique ways of selecting 3 nodes out of 6.) The solutions in this figure are lexicographically ordered. That is, the first solution is (A, B, C), the second is (A, B, D), the third is (A, B, E), and so on. Therefore, each solution in the figure differs from its immediate neighbor by exactly one value. Figure 2.5 is built in a similar way using the minimum node dissimilarity values.

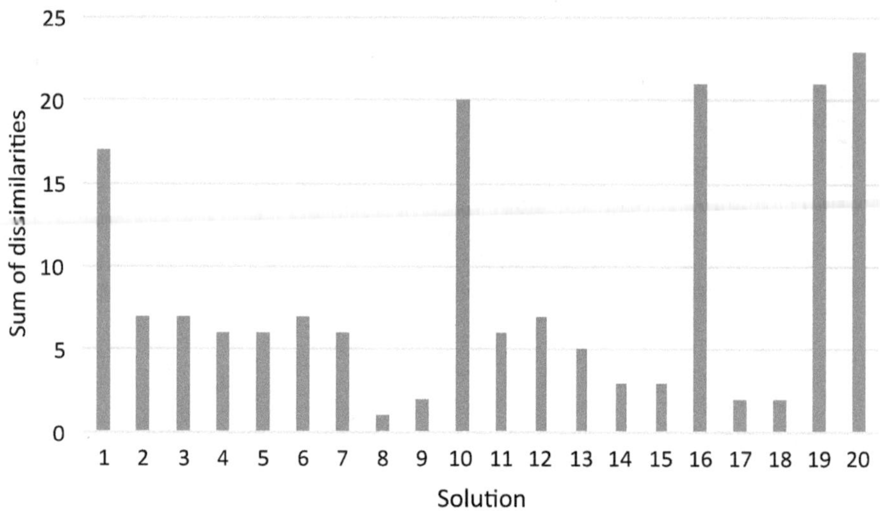

Fig. 2.4 Landscape of the sum of dissimilarities

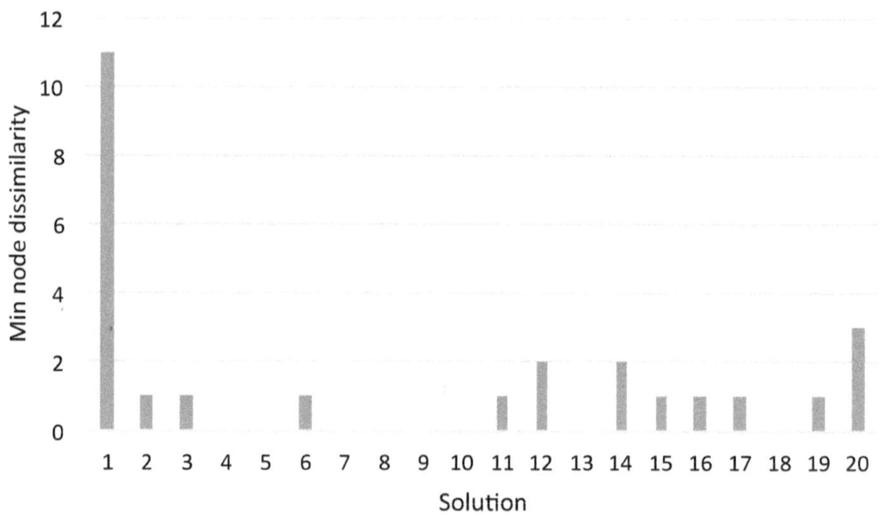

Fig. 2.5 Landscape of the minimum node dissimilarities

In the optimization jargon, the second objective function (see Fig. 2.5) is said to have a “flat” landscape. The flatness refers to a relatively large number of solutions with the same objective function value. In this case, 40% of the solutions (8 out of 20) have a value of zero. Spaces with flat landscapes are difficult to search because solutions are often surrounded by neighbors that have the same objective function value as the solution under consideration (also known as the current solution). That is, the objective function is not helpful for guiding the search and providing a direction where to move next. It is typical for a flat landscape to include one solution that clearly dominates all others, as in the case of Fig. 2.5, where the first solution (which is the global optimal) is significantly better than all the other ones.

The landscape in Fig. 2.4, on the other hand, is much more search-friendly. It includes 4 high quality solutions (10, 16, 19, and 20) and a relatively small percentage of solutions with the same value in a given region. While searching in a flat landscape is similar to trying to find a “needle in a haystack”, searching in a space with an associated rugged landscape makes the use of the objective function a valuable tool for finding search directions. Landscape analysis (even a basic one) is recommended in order to identify effective search mechanisms and to select the right methods and strategies. Generally, flat landscapes suggest that a search method should favor construction of solutions over neighborhood explorations.

2.3 Constraint Handling

Constraints are common in optimization problems. Arguably, all optimization problems include constraints in one way or another. In this section, however, we focus on constraints that require special attention and that cannot be implicitly taken into consideration by a clever choice of a solution representation. Let us explore this notion by revisiting Example 2.1. As stated, the problem has two constraints:

1. There are five sales representatives and therefore exactly five regions must be selected.
2. The company wishes to visit the doctors in all counties, therefore all counties must be “covered” by at least one region.

The first is a so-called “equality” constraint because feasible solutions must choose exactly five regions. The second is a “greater than or equal” constraint because the number of regions covering a county must be “at least” one. The binary solution representation does not implicitly account for either one of these constraints and therefore the solution procedure must be designed to handle them. Let us define a binary decision variable x_i to represent the choice of whether or not region i is selected. That is, $x_i = 1$ if region i is selected and zero otherwise. A solution to the problem is then represented as follows:

$$(x_1, x_2, \ldots, x_{10})$$

Give the two constraints in the problem, a feasible solution must satisfy the following equations:

$$
\begin{aligned}
&x_1 + x_2 + x_3 + x_4 + x_5 + x_6 + x_7 + x_8 + x_9 + x_{10} = 5 \\
&x_1 + x_3 + x_5 \geq 1 \\
&x_2 + x_4 + x_6 + x_8 \geq 1 \\
&x_1 + x_3 + x_7 + x_{10} \geq 1 \\
&x_2 + x_4 + x_9 \geq 1 \\
&x_1 + x_5 + x_8 \geq 1 \\
&x_2 + x_6 + x_{10} \geq 1 \\
&x_3 + x_7 + x_9 \geq 1 \\
&x_2 + x_5 + x_8 \geq 1 \\
&x_4 + x_7 + x_9 \geq 1 \\
&x_3 + x_6 + x_{10} \geq 1
\end{aligned}
$$

The first equation enforces exactly 5 of the binary variables to be one in any feasible solution. The following 10 equations enforce the coverage of the counties, with one equation corresponding to one county. For example, the first county can be covered by the selection of either region 1, 3, or 5. The second county can be covered by the selection of either one of four regions: 2, 4, 6, and 8. The interpretation of the other 8 equations is similar. If the problem is modeled this way, a solution procedure, when selecting regions, must verify that the selection satisfies all of these equations.

In the metaheuristic literature, the sequencing problem in Example 2.2 is considered unconstrained. Solutions are represented by a permutation vector and any permutation is a solution to the problem. However, if we model the problem by defining a decision variable x_i to indicate the identity of the job that will be processed in position i, the permutation representation implicitly handles the constraint that all x values must be different from each other. In other words, for the sequencing problem of Example 2.2, the permutation representation solves a problem that can be expressed as:

Decision variables: x_1, x_2, x_{10},
$1 \leq x_i \leq 10$ for $i = 1, \ldots, 10$,
All different.

There are three main constraint handling strategies used within metaheuristic methodologies: rejection, penalization, and repair. The **rejection** strategy consists of discarding any solution that does not meet all the constraints. For instance, suppose that in the problem of Example 2.1 a metaheuristic search is examining the solution (1, 2, 3, 5, 6), where the numbers represent the selected regions. The first constraint is clearly satisfied because the set consists of five distinct regions. The procedure then must examine whether the solution meets all the covering constraints. This examination reveals that all counties are cover by at least one region, except the 9th county. This county can be covered by regions 4, 7, and 9, but none of these regions has been selected in the trial solution under examination. If a rejection strategy is in place, the solution is then discarded. The downside of rejection is that the procedure does not "learn" anything about the infeasibility related to the discarded solution. Also, since the solution is discarded and there is no record that the solution was already examined, the strategy could result in a situation where the search is just "spinning wheels" instead of making progress toward finding high quality solutions. In general, a rejection strategy is only used when the percentage of infeasible solutions in the search space is relatively small.

Penalization is the process by which the value of an infeasible solution is altered by a function that imposes a penalty for violating problem constraints. Let the objective function value for a solution x be given by $f(x)$. Then, a linear penalty function has the following form:

$$f'(x) = f(x) + p \times c(x)$$

In this penalized objective function value $f'(x)$, the value of p is the penalty factor and $c(x)$ represents a measure of constraint violation associated with solution x. Note that for feasible solution $c(x) = 0$ and therefore $f'(x) = f(x)$. The penalty factor must be such that no infeasible solution ends up with a $f'(x)$ value that is better (i.e., smaller in a minimization problem or larger in a maximization problem) than the objective function value of a feasible solution. A special form of penalization that is in a sense equivalent to the rejection strategy consists of assigning to all infeasible solutions in a minimization problem a very large $f'(x)$ value (denoted by `LARGE`) in the following way:

$$f'(x) = \begin{cases} f(x) & \text{if } x \text{ is feasible} \\ \texttt{LARGE} & \text{if } x \text{ is infeasible} \end{cases}$$

A negative large value is assigned when the goal is to maximize the objective function value. This special form does not distinguish among infeasible solutions and has no capacity to exploit information related to solutions that are "close" to being feasible.

An appropriate value of p is typically found through experimentation. Knowledge of the problem context also helps in the selection of penalty factors. Referring back to Example 2.1, let us assume that the search process is set up in such a way that all the solutions that it generates are feasible with respect to the selection of regions. That is, the process produces solutions for which there are always five different regions selected. Now, we would like to use a penalty function to distinguish between the solutions that are feasible with respect to county coverage and the ones that are not. Also assume that we are using the range of the number of doctors assigned to each selected region as the objective function value. To find a suitable value for p, we can calculate a value that we know no feasible solution will ever reach. The problem data (see Table 2.1) show that county 4 has the smallest number of doctors (52). The data also show that there are 1,050 doctors in total. Therefore, the maximum possible range would be the result of assigning county 4 to one sales representative and all the other counties to another representative. The range value is the $1,050 - 52 = 998$. This is a very conservative value for the range, because we know that there are five sales representative and not just two. However, it is an easy calculation that does not involve additional analysis and refinements. If in addition, we define $c(x)$ as the number of uncovered counties, then the penalized objective function for Example 2.1 has the following form:

$$f'(x) = f(x) + 998 \times c(x)$$

This function guarantees that all infeasible solutions will have a penalized objective function value that is larger than the objective function value of any feasible solution. The smallest value of the penalty term is 998 and it occurs when $c(x) = 1$.

The constraints in Example 2.1 are of a special type that indicate whether or not a county is covered. Covering a county by more than one region does not provide information on the degree of feasibility of a solution. If a county is not covered, the left hand side of the equation is zero and this is true for all uncovered counties. Hence, there is no information that can be obtained from a single constraint on the degree of infeasibility of the solution being examined. The only meaningful information is the number of counties that are uncovered and this is why we defined $c(x)$ the way we did above.

There are constrained optimization problems for which a constraint that is violated can produce information on the degree of the violation. Consider a constraint for which the left hand side represents resources (e.g., money, people, machines, etc.) used by a solution x, denoted by $r(x)$, and the right hand side is a limit on the available resources, denoted by b. Then, the violation v of the constraint can be calculated as follows:

$$r(x) \leq b + v$$

In this case, v is an absolute violation value that is zero if the resources $r(x)$ needed by the solution x do not exceed the budget b. A relative measure could be more effective in situations where the problem contains multiple constraints with a ranges of values that are significantly different. A relative measure could have the following form:

$$r(x) \leq b(1 + v)$$

The advantage of a relative measure is that all the violation values are expressed as a fraction of the b values. This assumes that all violations are equally important unless individual p values are used for each constraint violation. A simple penalty function can be formulated by calculating $c(x)$ as the sum of the violations (either absolute or relative).

Repair strategies consist of the transformation of an infeasible solution into a feasible solution. The goal of a repair procedure should be to create a feasible solution out of an infeasible solution while keeping the feasible solution "as close as possible" as the originating infeasible solution. In other words, the idea is to make the least number of changes to the infeasible solution while transforming it into a feasible solution. Another goal, perhaps equally important as the first one, is that the transformation produces a feasible solution of the highest possible quality. Therefore, when changing elements or altering variable values to move an infeasible solution toward the feasibility region, the transformation rules should take advantage of problem context to make changes with the highest merit according to the objective function value. Greedy approaches that transform infeasible solutions into feasible solution one step at a time attempt to make changes that either improve the most or deteriorate the least the objective function value of the infeasible solution being transformed.

Example 2.5 Consider the region selection problem of Example 2.1. Assume that the objective function is the variance of the number of doctors in each of the selected regions. An optimization process produces the solution (1, 2, 3, 5, 6), which as stated above, it is infeasible because county 9 is not covered by any of the selected regions. Table 2.4 shows the characteristics of this solution.

Table 2.4 Characteristics of (1, 2, 3, 5, 6) solution

Region	Counties covered by selected region				Doctors
1	1	3	5		157
2	2	4	6	8	202
3	1	3	7		232
5	1	5	8		161
6	2	6	10		170

The objective function value of the solution in Table 2.4 is 820.74. Suppose that the repair procedure is such that it replaces, one at a time, selected regions with unselected regions until the solution becomes feasible. In order to repair this solution following such a process, we must identify candidate regions capable of covering the uncovered county 9. The candidates are regions 4, 7, and 9. We now could try all replacements and keep the one that repairs the solution and has the best objective function value. There are 15 possible replacement, as shown in Table 2.5. All but one of the resulting solutions are feasible. Solution 3 is not feasible because it does not cover county 7, which was covered only by region 3 in the original solution and this region is replaced by region 4 that does not include county 7 in the set of counties that it can cover.

Table 2.5 Solutions obtained by the repair procedure

Solution	Selected regions					Objective function value
1	2	3	4	5	6	3104.00
2	1	3	4	5	6	791.73
3	1	2	4	5	6	(*)527.67
4	1	2	3	4	6	1472.77
5	1	2	3	4	5	2645.17
6	2	3	5	6	7	778.30
7	1	3	5	6	7	1891.91
8	1	2	5	6	7	1001.90
9	1	2	3	6	7	851.80
10	1	2	3	5	7	3116.60
11	2	3	5	6	9	1336.30
12	1	3	5	6	9	1520.73
13	1	2	5	6	9	752.30
14	1	2	3	6	9	757.40
15	1	2	3	5	9	2460.47

*Infeasible solution, county 7 is not covered by any of the selected regions

The repair procedure, as performed in Table 2.5, identifies the replacement of region 5 with region 9 as the best change to transform the infeasible solution (1, 2, 3, 5, 6) with objective function value of 820.74 into the feasible solution (1, 2, 5, 6, 9) with objective function value of 752.30. In this case, a feasible solution was obtained by performing one step of the repair procedure. In larger problems, the repair procedure might need more than one step. In such a case, an infeasibility measure is needed to be able to choose moves that take the current solution closer to the feasibility region. In this example, we are able to select solution 13 in Table 2.5 solely based on its objective function value because there are several feasible solutions from which to choose. In the absence of a feasible solution, the rule should be such that the solution that is "least infeasible" should be chosen. We point out that repair mechanisms may fail even when the selection rule attempts to minimize the infeasibility of the current solution. In such a case, the solution may be discarded.

Some metaheuristic methods are designed to preserve feasibility. This means that once a feasible solution is found, the procedure makes only those moves that transform one feasible solution into another. For instance, in Example 2.5, once the search moves to solution (1, 2, 5, 6, 9), a feasibility preserving method would consider only those moves that replace regions in such a way that the resulting set covers all the counties. For efficiency purposes, the procedure would first verify the feasibility of the move (in this case, the replacement of a region) and then it would calculate the objective function value of the resulting solution as long as it is feasible.

2.4 Design Choices and Parameter Tuning

Metaheuristic methodologies provide a framework to create procedures to search for high quality solutions in spaces defined by the formulation of optimization problems. There are two main search spaces: discrete and continuous. Discrete spaces are typically associated with combinatorial optimization problems, for example, those for which the decision variables are represented by a set of discrete values, a binary, or a permutation vector. Continuous spaces are defined by a set of real (continuous) variables. There are also complex problems that involve mixed search spaces characterized by a combination of discrete and continuous variables.

Researchers have concluded that no single methodology is capable of dominating any other one in all problem settings and search spaces. While there is no scientific way of showing that one methodology is better than another one in general, the scientific process can be applied to show that a procedure emanating from a metaheuristic framework can perform better than another procedure, from the same metaheuristic framework or another one, in a particular class of problems. This means that when comparing solution methods, we are not comparing methodologies but rather particular implementations of methodological frameworks.

Each metaheuristic methodology includes a set of strategy and a general "search philosophy." As mentioned in Chap. 1, some methodologies are based on exploring the search space by moving from one solution to another. Other methodologies construct and maintain a population of solutions that continue to change (evolve) in stages. This evolution occurs according to rules and strategies to transform solutions and to include and discard them from the population. There are differences within single-solution based methodologies in the same way that not all the population-based methodologies are the same. For example, some rely more in randomization than others.

An instantiation of a methodology is its application to a particular problem or class of problems. Two applications of the same methodology to the same problem does not necessarily result in the same search procedure. The reason is that a metaheuristic implementation is the result of design choices and parameter tuning. The analyst decides which elements from the methodology to include in the implementation and how these elements will interact. The analyst also decides how to calibrate the performance of his/her implementation and therefore how to adjust the parameter values that ultimately determine the efficiency of the procedure.

Example 2.6 Consider the sequencing problem in Example 2.2 and assume that we want to optimize the nonregular objective function that penalizes both earliness and tardiness. Specifically, let p_j and d_j be the processing time and the due date, respectively, of job j. Also, let s be a solution to the problem represented as the ordering of the jobs. That is, s is a permutation for which $s(j)$ is the index of the job in position j. Then, the just-in-time objective function can be formulated as follows:

$$f(s) = \sum_{j=1}^{n} |c(s(j)) - d(s(j))|$$

In this formula, $c(s(j))$ represents the completion time of job in position j in the sequence, and $||$ is the absolute value function. This means that either positive or negative deviations from the due date count equally toward the total sum. The completion time of the job in position j is calculated with the following formula:

$$c(s(j)) = \sum_{i=1}^{j} p(s(i))$$

What this formula states is that the completion time for a job in position j is given by the sum of the processing time of all the jobs in positions before j plus the processing time of the job in position j. Table 2.6 shows the calculation of the objective function value of the solution given by ordering the jobs in Table 2.2 by increasing value of their due dates. This ordering is called the EDD (earliest due date) rule in the scheduling literature and in this case results in $s = (1, 3, 5, 4, 2, 6, 7, 8, 10, 9)$.

Table 2.6 Objective function value for EDD solution

Job	Processing	Due date	Completion	Deviation
1	10	12	10	2
3	7	20	17	3
5	3	23	20	3
4	5	27	25	2
2	11	35	36	1
6	7	36	43	7
7	5	40	48	8
8	5	40	53	13
10	11	47	64	17
9	12	55	76	21
Objective function value:				77

The jobs in Table 2.6 are EDD ordered, as seen by the increasing values in the due date column. The completion time is the accumulated processing time, including all previous jobs and the current job. The deviation is the absolution difference between the due date and the completion time. Finally, the objective function value is the sum of all completions.

One of the first design decisions that an analysis faces is how to initialize the search. For instance, Analyst A might decide that the search will start from a random solution, which in Example 2.6 would correspond to a random sequence. Analyst B, who could be basing his/her implementation on the same methodology as the Analyst A, might decide to initiate the search from the EDD solution shown in

Table 2.6. Both procedures, A and B, could be based on the same principles but the initialization of the search has been implanted in two different ways and therefore could lead to different results.

Then, the analysts must decide how solutions are going to be transformed during the search. This transformation process is referred to as a move mechanism, or simply a **move**. Two typical moves in permutation spaces are insertions and swaps. An **insertion** is the transferring of a single job from its current position to a new one. For instance, consider the solution in Table 2.6. Job 5 is currently in position 3, as shown in the following solution representation:

$$(1, 3, 5, 4, 2, 6, 7, 8, 10, 9)$$

An insertion move that takes job 5 from its current position and moves it to the sixth position results in the following solution:

$$(1, 3, 4, 2, 6, 5, 7, 8, 10, 9)$$

Note that this move caused jobs 4, 2, and 6 to "shift to the left" one position. These jobs used to be in position 4, 5, and, 6, but now they are in positions 3, 4, and 5. As intended, job 5 now occupies position 6. The objective function associated with the new solution is 95. As defined in Sect. 1.3, the move value is the difference between the objective function value before the move and the objective function value after the move. In this example, the move value is 18. Since the goal is to minimize the objective function value, a positive move value indicates a move to an inferior solution.

Now, let us consider a swap instead of an insert. A swap is an exchange of the positions of two elements (jobs, in our example). For instance, the swap of jobs 5 and 6 in the solution of Table 2.6 results in the following solution:

$$(1, 3, 6, 4, 2, 5, 7, 8, 10, 9)$$

The objective function associated with this solution is 103 for a move value of 26. A search procedure does not have to be limited to either swaps of inserts. For example, a procedure could be designed to perform inserts for a number of initial search steps and then perform swaps for the remainder of the search. Another design could be such that inserts and swaps alternate with certain periodicity. There are many different design choices even for a relatively simple search such as the one illustrated here.

When design choices involve parameters, a tuning process is necessary to configure a procedure. A **search parameter** is an input value to the procedure that is controlled by the analyst and that has an effect on the behavior of the procedure and ultimately on its efficiency and effectiveness. For instance, in the job sequencing problem, a parameter `INIT` could indicate the number of initial iterations (i.e., moves executed during the search) in which the procedure is going to perform inserts before permanently switching to performing swap as a mechanism to search the solution space. The value of `INIT` might not be immediately obvious and careful experimentation is typically necessary to find effective search parameter values.

Referring back to our Chap. 1 discussion on model simplicity and elegance, as a general rule, the simpler models are those with fewer adjustable parameters. The more parameters the harder it is to find a combination of values that make the procedure work well across many instances of the problem that is designed to solve. It is not hard to begin with a simple deign and rapidly move to levels of complexity that require more and more parameters. For instance, one possibility in the sequencing problem is to limit the "jump" that any job makes in a single move. The jump is the difference between the current position of the job and the position that occupies after the move. Limiting the jump could improve the efficiency of the solution procedure, since it is unlikely that transferring a job too far from a position that is natural for its due date will result in a high-quality solution. While the rationale makes sense, the implementation adds a layer of complexity since we now will need to adjust a parameter `JUMP` indicating the maximum distance (measured in terms of number of positions) that a job is allowed to travel in a single move.

Compromises are often quite effective in implementing a sound idea and avoiding the added complexity. For instance, inserts and swaps in the sequencing problem could be limited to immediate positions. This is the same as setting `JUMP` equal to one. The effect of such a choice is twofold. On one hand, the `JUMP` parameter is no longer an adjustable value. And, on the other hand, the size of the neighborhood (i.e., the number of moves to explore around a given solution) decreases. When jobs are only allowed to move no more than one position away from its current position, inserts and swaps are equivalent, rendering the parameter `INIT` unnecessary. The number of moves is given by $n - 1$, where n is the number of jobs. However, when the distance is not limited at all (i.e., `JUMP` is set to n), the number of swaps is given by the following formula:

$$\frac{n^2 - n}{2}$$

Therefore, there are 45 possible swaps in a problem with 10 jobs, but there are only 9 swaps of jobs that are in immediate positions. The nine neighboring solutions that can be reached from the solution in Table 2.6 are shown in Table 2.7. The first row shows the current solution and the following nine rows show the neighbors that can be reached by performing swaps of jobs in immediate positions. The neighbors are labeled N1 to N9, assuming a so-called lexicographic ordering of the swap exploration.

As shown in Table 2.7, the swap of jobs 6 and 7 is the best move with a value of –2, because the objective function value (last column in the table, labeled *O.F.*) decreases from 77 to 75. This swap results in the solution labeled as N6 and highlighted in bold in Table 2.7. A design issue related to the exploration of a neighborhood relates to the order in which the moves are examined. This is relevant when the neighborhoods are very large (i.e., when they include many moves) and a

first-improving strategy is implemented. This strategy consists of executing a move as soon as an improvement is identified. For example, consider the neighborhood in Table 2.7. The procedure starts by swapping the jobs in positions 1 and 2 to examine the first neighbor (labeled N1). Then, it swaps the jobs in positions 2 and 3 to examine N2. In the first-improving strategy, the procedure will stop the neighborhood exploration as soon as it reaches N6 because this neighbor is better than the current solution. The move is executed and the search moves to solution N6. That is, N6 becomes the new current solution. The next exploration starts by attempting to swap the jobs in positions 7 and 8. Then, it continues with 8 and 9, 9 and 10, and it "wraps around" to 1 and 2. This creates a circular list for the ordering of the exploration. The process stops either when an improvement is found or when the entire 9 moves have been explored and no improvement has been identified. At this point, a decision, which depends on the methodology being applied, is made to move the search to another point.

Table 2.7 Reduced swap neighborhood

Solution	Sequence										O.F.
Current	1	3	5	4	2	6	7	8	10	9	77
N1	3	1	5	4	2	6	7	8	10	9	90
N2	1	5	3	4	2	6	7	8	10	9	81
N3	1	3	4	5	2	6	7	8	10	9	79
N4	1	3	5	2	4	6	7	8	10	9	87
N5	1	3	5	4	6	2	7	8	10	9	81
N6	**1**	**3**	**5**	**4**	**2**	**7**	**6**	**8**	**10**	**9**	**75**
N7	1	3	5	4	2	6	8	7	10	9	77
N8	1	3	5	4	2	6	7	10	8	9	83
N9	1	3	5	4	2	6	7	8	9	10	78

*Infeasible solution, county 7 is not covered by any of the selected regions

The best-improving strategy is an alternative to first-improving. In best improving, the order of the exploration is not important because all moves are evaluated and a decision where to go next is made after the quality of all neighbors has been determined. The advantage of a first-improving strategy is that the search has the potential to move faster to a new solution, without the need for evaluating the entire neighborhood. The disadvantage is that a large improvement might be missed due to the ordering in which the moves are explored. On the other hand, the advantage of the best-improving strategy is that the largest improvement is always identified, moving the search more rapidly to a local optimum. The disadvantage is that, for large neighborhoods, identifying the best improving move requires a considerable amount of computational resources.

Researchers have dealt and continue to deal with issues related to design choices and parameter tuning. Much of the effort has been applied to developing automated systems that could perform these tasks with little or no human involvement.

Automated tuning systems have been proposed based on the general area of design of experiments. These systems search for the combination of parameter values that make the procedure more likely to perform at its highest level when tackling a given class of problems. CALIBRA[1] is an example of a parameter tuning system based on experimental design procedures (see [1]). A step further in this line of research includes systems that not only search for the best combination of parameter values but also for the best combination of search elements. In other words, the analysts do not have to commit to a particular design or strategy (e.g., selecting between first-improving and best-improving) and instead they may include all choices and let an automated design engine select what is best for particular problem classes and at particular stages of the search process. Programming by Optimization, PbO,[2] is a prominent example of such a system (see [2]:

> "Premature commitment to design choices during software development often leads to loss of performance and limited flexibility. Programming by Optimization (PbO) is a design paradigm that aims to avoid such premature design choices and to actively develop promising alternatives for parts of the design. Rather than building a single program for a given purpose, software developers specify a rich and potentially large design space of programs. From this specification, programs that perform well in a given context are generated automatically through optimization techniques. PbO allows human experts to focus on the creative task of imagining possible mechanisms for solving given problems or subproblems, while the tedious job of determining what works best in a particular context is performed automatically, substituting human labor with computation."

Research in this area will continue, fueled by the promising results obtained by systems such as PbO. What seems to be clear at the moment is that the task of designing strategies and procedural elements that can be used to search solution spaces will still be the responsibility of a human analyst.

2.5 Exercises

1. The following questions relate to the problem described in Example 2.1:
   a. Develop a spreadsheet model of the problem using the binary representation of the decision variables and the variance of the number of doctors assigned to each region as the objective function. Use the `VAR.P` formula to calculate the variance.
   b. Verify that the spreadsheet model is correct by checking that the solution (0, 1, 1, 0, 1, 1, 1, 0, 0, 0) results in a variance of 778.3.
   c. Use the Evolutionary Solver in Excel to search for a high quality solution to this problem. Note that that an optimization model needs to be formulated in order to use the Evolutionary Solver. This entails declaring an objective

[1] http://coruxa.epsig.uniovi.es/~adenso/file_d.html.

[2] http://www.prog-by-opt.net/.

function, an optimization goal (maximize or minimize), a set of decision variables (changing cells), and constraints. What solution do you obtain?
d. On a new spreadsheet, develop a spreadsheet model using the discrete-value representation of the decision variables and the variance of the number of doctors assigned to each region as the objective function. Use the `VAR.P` formula to calculate the variance.
e. Verify that the spreadsheet model is correct by checking that the solution (2, 3, 5, 6, 7) results in a variance of 778.3.
f. Use the Evolutionary Solver in Excel to search for a high quality solution to this problem. Compare the solution obtained with this model and the solution obtained with the binary model.

2. The following questions relate to the problem in Example 2.2:

    a. Develop a spreadsheet model of the problem by creating 10 cells for the processing ordering. That is, these cells represent a permutation of the jobs and therefore they represent the solution to the problem.
    b. In three separate cells, calculate the following performance metrics: (1) number of tardy jobs, (2) total tardiness (i.e., the sum of all days by which jobs are tardy), and (3) total tardiness plus total earliness (i.e., the sum of all the days by which completion times deviate from the due dates).
    c. Verify that the spreadsheet model is correct by checking that the solution (1, 3, 5, 4, 2, 6, 7, 8, 9, 10) results in 6 tardy jobs, a total tardiness of 68, and total deviation from the dues dates of 78.
    d. Use the Evolutionary Solver in Excel to search for a high quality solution to this problem. Note that an "All different" (dif) constraint must be specified to declare that the decision variables represent a permutation. Run the solver three times, once for each of the objective functions. Compare the solutions found by these three executions of the solver.

3. Figure 2.6 shows ten elements represented by nodes that are labeled A to J. An edge between a pair of nodes indicates the degree of the dissimilarity between the nodes connected to the edge. The larger the value the more dissimilar the elements that are connected by the edge. The problem consists of selecting 5 elements in order to maximize a measure of dissimilarity. Two measures are being considered: (1) the sum of the dissimilarities of all the selected elements and (2) the minimum node dissimilarity, where the dissimilarity of a node is the sum of all the dissimilarities of the selected nodes connected to it. This situation may arise when selecting a team out of a pool of individuals. The goal is to select a diverse team, where diversity between two individuals may be a value that summarizes differences such as gender, ethnicity, level of education, or national origin. Selecting a team guided by the first diversity measure described above produces a set of individuals that collectively are the most diverse. However, the solution could result in a team where only a few individuals are very diverse with respect to each other, with the rest of them being fairly similar. Maximizing the

second diversity measure avoids this situation and creates some diversity equity among all team members.

a. Develop a spreadsheet model of the problem using a binary representation for the decision variables and creating objective function cells for both dissimilarity measures.
b. Verify that the spreadsheet model is correct by checking that the solution (A, B, G, I, J) results in a total dissimilarity of 11 and a minimum node dissimilarity of 2, corresponding to element J.
c. Use the Evolutionary Solver in Excel to search for a high quality solution to this problem. First find a high quality solution with respect to the first objective function and then find one with respect to the second objective function. Are these solutions the same?

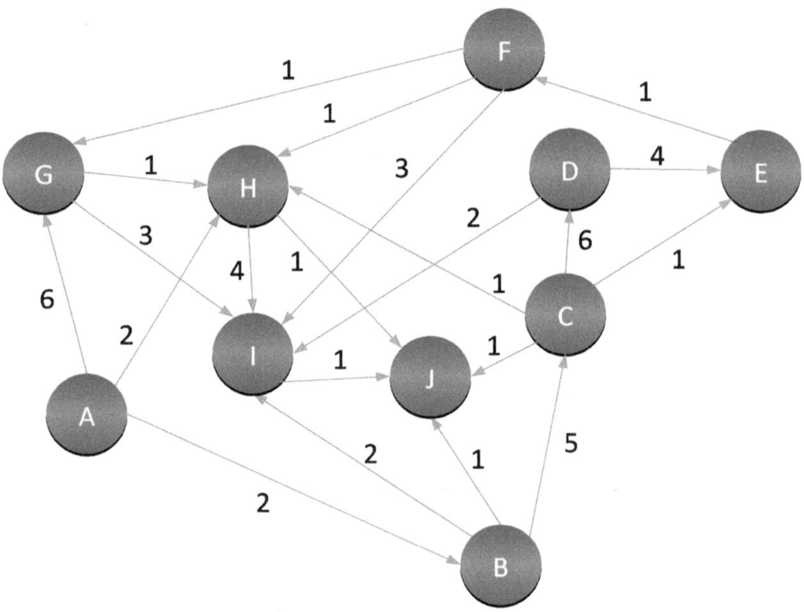

Fig. 2.6 Graph for Exercise 3

4. (Adapted from [4]). A small but growing company in the food industry is considering entering the breakfast market. In particular, it would like to add cold cereal products. Before developing its own line of cereals, the company wants to identify if there are different market segments. Specifically, the company would like to figure out if there is a health-conscious segment and a taste segment. The company has collected per-serving nutritional profiles for 74 different cold cereals currently in the market. The nutritional profile consists of the values of nine nutritional components: calories, protein, fat, sodium, fiber, carbs, sugar, potas-

sium, and vitamins. The data are in the *Exercise2-4.xlsx* file that accompanies this book. The problem of identifying market segments is typically approached with a technique known as cluster analysis, which is one of the data mining tools in business analytics. Cluster analysis consists of grouping observations into clusters and measuring the distance between the observations in each cluster. The goal is to find clusters of observations that share similar attributes. The merit of a particular clustering is typically measured by the total distance between each observation and its cluster centroid. The centroid of a cluster is the average value of each attribute for all the observations assigned to the cluster.

a. Develop a spreadsheet model of the problem using a binary representation for the decision variables and creating an objective function cell that calculates the total distance between each observation and the centroid of the cluster to which it is assigned. Note that there are 74 decision variables in this problem, one for each observation. A zero indicates that the observation is assigned to cluster 0 and a one indicates that the observation is assigned to cluster 1.
b. Verify that the spreadsheet model is correct by checking that the solution that assigns the first 37 observations to cluster 0 and the remaining observations to cluster 1 results in a total distance of 12,774.6.
c. Use the Evolutionary Solver in Excel to search for a high quality solution to this problem. Compare the Nutritional profiles of the centroids of the clusters in the best solution found by the solver. Can you identify two different market segments?

References

1. Adenso-Díaz, B., and M. Laguna. 2006. Fine-tuning of algorithms using partial experimental designs and local search. *Operations Research* 54 (1): 99–114.
2. Hoos, H.H. 2012. Programming by optimization. *Communications of the ACM* 55 (2): 70–80.
3. Laguna, M., J. Molina, F. Pérez, R. Caballero, and A. Hernández-Díaz, 2010. The challenge of optimizing expensive black boxes: a scatter search/rough set theory approach. *Journal of the Operational Research Society* 61 (1): 53–67.
4. Ragsdale, C. 2015. *Spreadsheet modeling and decision analysis: a practical introduction to business analytics*. Boston: Cengage Learning.
5. Talbi, E-G. 2009. *Metaheuristics: From design to implementation*. New Jersey: Wiley.

Chapter 3
Greedy Randomized Adaptive Search Procedures

3.1 Motivation

In this chapter, we describe the process of designing heuristic procedures to solve combinatorial optimization problems. Most combinatorial optimization problems are relatively easy to formulate in mathematical terms, but can be very difficult to solve, because they include non-linear or integer constraints. In most cases, if we want to solve them using a spreadsheet, such as Microsoft Excel, the only option is to use a metaheuristics-based solver, such as the evolutionary solving method in Excel. However, often this type of black-box solver provides relatively low-quality solutions. This chapter offers an alternative approach consisting of designing a specific solver for a problem. We will see how a relatively simple procedure, specifically created for a given problem, is able to render high-quality solutions. In particular, in this chapter we will design a method based on the GRASP methodology (i.e., a Greedy Randomized Adaptive Search Procedure). In subsequent chapters, we will apply other methodologies to design heuristic solution methods.

Example 3.1 Consider a group of 100 university students from which we want to select five to form a committee. For each pair of students, we can compute a distance value based on their particular attributes. These include personal characteristics such as age, gender, or religion, and academic skills such as creative abilities, knowledge of disciplines, or leadership, to mention a few. A pair of students with similar attributes receives a low distance value, while students with different attributes have a large distance value. To create a diverse committee, the five students have to be selected in a way that their ten pairwise distances are relatively large. The most diverse committee would represent the maximum sum of the distances between the selected students. In this chapter, we explain different ways for obtaining a good selection of five diverse students. The file *MDP1.xlsx* contains the distance values for this example.

A. Duarte et al., *Metaheuristics for Business Analytics*, EURO Advanced Tutorials on Operational Research, https://doi.org/10.1007/978-3-319-68119-1_3

Maximizing diversity involves selecting a subset of elements from a given set in a way that the diversity among the elements is as large as possible. Several models have been proposed to address this combinatorial optimization problem. All of them require a diversity measure, typically a distance function. The definition of this distance between elements (students in our example) depends on each specific application. Diversity models are used in many areas, including plant breeding, social problems, ecological preservation, pollution control, product design, capital investment, workforce management, curriculum design, and genetic engineering. Therefore, the methods and techniques described in this chapter are not limited to our specific example, but they have a large domain of applications.

In this chapter, we focus on a well-known diversity model, the Max-Sum, in which we seek to maximize the sum of the distances between the selected elements. Note that other models could also be applied, such as maximizing the minimum distance between the selected elements. Using the Max-Sum model, our problem can be easily formulated in mathematical terms as follows:

Let $G=(V,E)$ denote a complete graph on n nodes, i.e., the graph with node set $V=\{1,2,\ldots,n\}$ and the property that for every pair of nodes i and j there is an edge $(i,j)\in E$. Additionally, each edge (i,j) has an associated value d_{ij}, which represents the inter-distance between the two nodes i and j. Let $M\subseteq V$ be the set of m selected elements. The graph is simply an abstract representation of our problem in which each node stands for an object or a person, and the edge distance shows the degree of similarity between the pairs of objects. We now formulate the diversity problem in terms of variables and constraints.

We define 0/1 variables x_i, $1\leq i\leq n$, where $x_i=1$ if node i is selected, and $x_i=0$ otherwise. Then, the Max-Sum diversity problem (MDP) can be formulated as a mathematical program as:

$$\max \quad \textstyle\sum_{i<j} d_{ij}x_ix_j \tag{3.1}$$

$$\textstyle\sum_{i=1} x_i = m \tag{3.2}$$

$$x_i \in \{0,1\}, 1\leq i\leq n. \tag{3.3}$$

This is the canonical formulation of the MDP. The set of the m selected elements is $M=\{i : x_i=1\}$ and the objective function, called $f(M)$, is the sum of the distances between the selected elements. Alternative formulations and models have been proposed for this problem, but for our purposes, this formulation is sufficient.

There is no single way of measuring diversity, and each of them gives rise to a different solution depending on the model used. We have identified five different measures to compute the diversity in M, which can be mapped into different objective functions in the above formulation. Table 3.1 summarizes them.

The different models in Table 3.1 illustrates an important fact: the same problem can be formulated in different ways. This is a major consideration when solving an optimization problem. Different models can lead to different solutions, and therefore we should carefully select the one that best reflects our objective. The following small example illustrates this. Let us consider that we have seven elements of which

Table 3.1 Diversity measures

Measure	Mathematical function	Description
Sum	$\sum_{i<j,i,j\in M} d_{ij}$	This is the standard diversification measure based on the sum of the distances.
Min	$\min_{i<j,i,j\in M} d_{ij}$	This measure is based on the minimum distance among the selected elements.
Mean	$\frac{\sum_{i<j,i,j\in M} d_{ij}}{\lvert M\rvert}$	Related to the Sum measure, this is an average equity measure.
Minsum	$\min_{i\in M} \sum_{j\in n, j\neq i} d_{ij}$	This measure considers the minimum aggregate dispersion among elements.
Diff	$\max_{i\in M} \sum_{j\in M, j\neq i} d_{ij} - \min_{i\in M} \sum_{j\in M, j\neq i} d_{ij}$	This measure computes the difference between the largest and smallest values of the dispersion sum.

we need to select five. Furthermore, the distances between each pair of elements are given by the matrix:

$$D = \begin{pmatrix} -- & 4.6 & 6.2 & 2.1 & 3.5 & 3.6 & 4.4 \\ 4.6 & -- & 6.6 & 7.1 & 8.2 & 2.4 & 5.3 \\ 6.2 & 6.6 & -- & 2.1 & 3.5 & 3.6 & 4.4 \\ 2.1 & 7.1 & 2.1 & -- & 5.5 & 1.1 & 2.3 \\ 3.5 & 8.2 & 3.5 & 5.5 & -- & 6.4 & 3.4 \\ 3.6 & 2.4 & 3.6 & 1.1 & 6.4 & -- & 5.4 \\ 4.4 & 5.3 & 4.4 & 2.3 & 3.4 & 5.4 & -- \end{pmatrix}.$$

For such a small example, we can enumerate all possible solutions (selections of elements) and compute the value of the Max-Sum DP and the value of the Max-Min DP for each one. The correlation between both objective functions is 0.61, which can be considered relatively low. Therefore, we should not expect a method for one of these problems to obtain good solutions for the other one. We extend now this analysis by including the Max-MinSum, Min-Diff, Max-Sum and Max-Min models (the Max-Mean model is not included because it does not set *a priori* the number of elements to select, as it is the case with the others), and we see in Table 3.2 that most of them are very low correlated. This table shows the correlations on 30 instances, with d_{ij} randomly generated with a uniform distribution in the range $[0, 20]$, $n = 20$, and $m = 5$.

We can implement any of the formulations in Table 3.1 in an Excel spreadsheet and apply one of its solvers to obtain a solution for a given instance. In particular, we consider the Max-Sum formulation (the first one in the table), and the data in the accompanying Excel file *MDP1.xlsx* corresponding to the distances of the 100 students in Example 3.1, from which we want to select five of them. In this file, the 100×100 distance matrix, $D = (d_{ij})$, is in the range A1:CV100, and the array x with the 100 binary variables, $x = (x_i)$, is in the range CX1:CX100.

Table 3.2 Correlations between different models

	Max-Sum	Max-Min	Max-MinSum	Min-Diff
Max-Sum	–	0.60	0.96	−0.17
Max-Min	–	–	0.73	−0.63
Max-MinSum	–	–	–	−0.44
Min-Diff	–	–	–	–

To compute the objective function, we have to add all the distances between the pairs of the selected elements. As the above mathematical formulation shows, we obtain this function by adding the expression $d_{ij}x_ix_j$, for all pairs of elements (i, j) such that $i < j$. In algebraic terms, the function is obtained from the expression $\frac{1}{2}x'Dx$, where x' represents the transpose of vector x. Note that in this expression, for each pair (i, j) we add up d_{ij} and d_{ji}. Since both quantities have the same value (we only consider here symmetrical distance matrices), i.e., $d_{ij} = d_{ji}$, we have to divide the result by 2. In short:

$$\frac{1}{2}x'Dx = \sum_{i<j,i,j\in V} d_{ij}x_ix_j. \tag{3.4}$$

This can be easily computed in Excel with the `MMULT(array1,array2)` function, which performs the matrix product between `array1` and `array2`. Note, however, that there are two products in our expression, and the x array first appears transposed. The Excel function `TRANSPOSE(CX1:CX100)` computes the transpose of x, which is in the range CX1:CX100. To multiply matrix D, which is in the range of A1:CV100, by the array x, we use the Excel function `MMULT(A1:CV100;CX1:CX100)`. Then, we multiply the transpose of x by the result of the previous multiplication. A drawback of the `MMULT()` function is that it can only multiply two matrices at the same time. However, we can *nest* it, which yields the following result:

```
{=MMULT(TRANSPOSE(CX1:CX100);MMULT(A1:CV100;CX1:CX100))/2}
```

You don't have to type this expression yourself! It is already computed in cell CZ3 of our Excel file, to provide you with the problem's objective function value. Note that if you want to type this expression (just for fun), you need to enter `MMULT()` as an *array formula*, not as a standard formula. This means that since it normally returns an array of values, rather than hit `Enter` when you type the formula, you have to press `Ctrl-Shift-Enter` and Excel will enter it as an array (inserting the brackets that contain the expression). Please note that you cannot enter these brackets manually. However, as mentioned above, this has already been done, and you can see the result in the MDP1.xlsx file.

To complete the model, we only need to add the constraint that limits the number of selected elements to m (5 in our example). As shown in the mathematical formulation above, it simply consists in the sum of the variables, which is obtained in Excel with the expression `=SUM(CX1:CX100)` (cell CZ6 of our file).

A feasible solution can easily be input in our model by, for example, entering 1 for the first 5 variables (i.e., in the cells in the range CX1:CX5). This results in a value of 141. Of course, we do not expect this solution to be good (i.e., to have a relatively high objective function value); we are simply providing the solving method with an initial solution. Figure 3.1 shows a partial view of our Excel file.

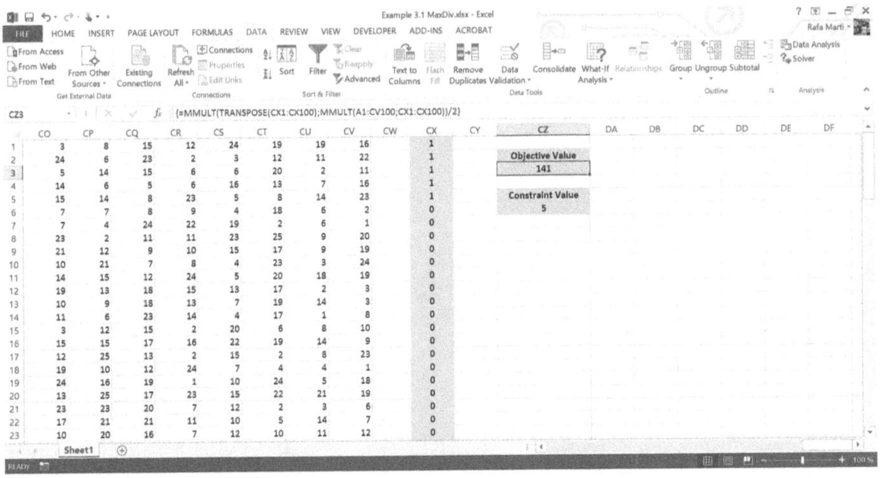

Fig. 3.1 Problem data and mathematical model

When all the elements (data, variables, objective function, and constraints) are set in the Excel file, we open the Solver to define the model. Figure 3.2 shows the Solver Parameters window, where we can identify these elements in our MDP model. Specifically, we can see the cell `CZ3` in the *Set Objective* field, the range `CX1:CX100` in the *By Changing Variable Cells* field, and two constraints in the *Subject to the Constraints* window. Note that in addition to the constraint limiting the number of selected elements to 5, `CZ6=5`, we have to include a constraint to set all variables to binary, `CX1:CX100=binary`. Finally, we set the *Select a Solving Method* option to *Evolutionary* and click *Solve*. After a few seconds, the solver engine based on Genetic Algorithms is able to improve the initial solution, generating a solution with a value of 204. If we run it longer, we can further improve this value. However, in the next section we will see how a simple method specifically designed for the MDP, is able to obtain a better solution in shorter running time.

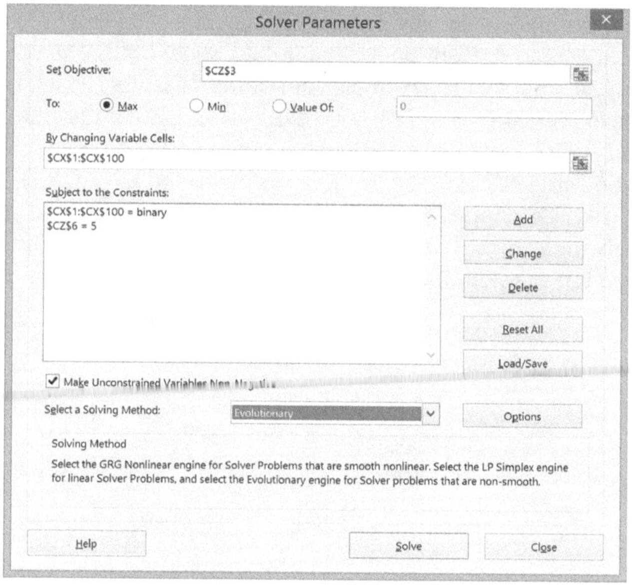

Fig. 3.2 The elements of the model in the Solver window

3.2 A Constructive Method

We will now describe a constructive heuristic, i.e., a method which follows a given principle for constructing solutions for the MDP by a sequence of steps. A construction could consist of a random selection of m elements from all n elements in the problem, but we cannot expect such a random solution to have a good value. The principle should somehow reflect that we are searching for a subset of elements with a large sum of distances. A good principle is then to select, at each step, the element with the maximum distance to the elements that have been already selected. We can implement this principle in an iterative process which, step by step, adds one element at a time, until m elements are selected.

We now describe an algorithm based on the above principle . Let $M \subseteq V$ be the set of selected elements. Initially, M is empty, and we add elements to M until it contains m elements (i.e., until $|M| = m$). For each element i, we first define an evaluation function, $cont(i)$, to measure its potential contribution to the partial solution under construction. Consider, for example, that the partial solution M which we are building contains three elements, denoted as 1, 2, and 3. The objective function value, or simply the value, of this partial solution is the sum of the distances between its elements (in mathematical terms: $f(M) = d_{12} + d_{13} + d_{23}$). If we add a new element to M, say element 9, then its value $f(M)$ would increase by the sum of the distances between the element 9 and the elements already in M, i.e., the elements 1, 2, and 3. We then define the potential contribution of element 9 as

$cont(9) = d_{19} + d_{29} + d_{39}$. In general terms, we define the contribution of an element i to a partial solution M as:

$$cont(i) = \sum_{j \in M} d_{ij}. \tag{3.5}$$

The objective of the MDP is to obtain a set M with the largest sum of distances between its elements. Therefore, it makes sense to select, at each iteration of our constructive method, the element i with the largest $cont(i)$ value. In particular, the method starts by selecting the two elements, s and t, with the largest distance between them, and the set M is initialized with them ($M = \{s,t\}$ and $f(M) = d_{st}$). Then, in subsequent iterations, the element i with the largest contribution is selected from the candidate set of elements, CL, which contains all non-selected elements ($CL = V \setminus M$). In mathematical terms, we select from CL the element i such that

$$cont(i) = \max_{j \in CL} cont(j). \tag{3.6}$$

Algorithm 1 shows a pseudo-code of our constructive method. Line 2 computes the two elements with the maximum distance, s and t. The sets M and CL are initialized in lines 3 and 4 respectively, together with the objective function value $f(M)$. The contribution value, $cont(j)$, is computed for all element $j \in CL$, as the sum of its distance to s and t (line 5). Lines 6 to 12 determine the main loop of the algorithm with the *while* command. The element i with the maximum contribution in CL is computed in line 7. Next, it is added to M and updated in line 8, while being removed from CL in line 9. Finally, the contribution value is updated in lines 10 and 11. The method continues until m elements have been selected (as determined in line 6).

Algorithm 1: Constructive method

1: Let $G = (V,E)$ be a graph with distance matrix $D = (d_{ij})$
2: $d_{st} \leftarrow \max_{(i,j) \in E} d_{ij}$
3: $M \leftarrow \{s,t\}$ and $f(M) = d_{st}$
4: $CL = V \setminus M$
5: $cont(j) = d_{js} + d_{jt} \; \forall j \in CL$
6: **while** $|M| < m$ **do**
7: $\quad i \leftarrow i \in CL \mid cont(i) = \max_{j \in CL} cont(j)$
8: $\quad M \leftarrow M \cup \{i\}$ and $f(M) = f(M) + cont(i)$
9: $\quad \mathrm{CL} \leftarrow \mathrm{CL} \setminus \{i\}$
10: $\quad cont(i) = 0$
11: $\quad cont(j) = cont(j) + d_{ij} \; \forall j \in CL$
12: **end while**
13: **return** M and $f(M)$

3.2.1 The Visual Basic Macro

We now implement Algorithm 1 in our Excel file to solve the Example 3.1. In particular, we code it in the Visual Basic language, creating a *Macro*. To start our code, we first have to create a command button to launch the Visual Basic editor.

To create a Visual Basic macro in the Excel file, the first step is to show the *Developer Tab* on the Ribbon by simply following these steps:

- On the *File tab*, choose the *Options* button.
- In the *ApplicationName* Options dialog box, click *Customize Ribbon.*
- In the list of main tabs, select the *Developer* check box.

Excel 2007 users, please remember that the *File* command means clicking the round button in the upper left. Then, in the Excel *Options* dialog box, select *Popular*, and place a check mark next to *Show Developer tab* in the Ribbon. Finally, click OK to see the new Developer tab displayed in the Ribbon. From the *Developer* ribbon click on the *Macro Security* button. Check the second level *Disable all Macros with Notification* and you are set.

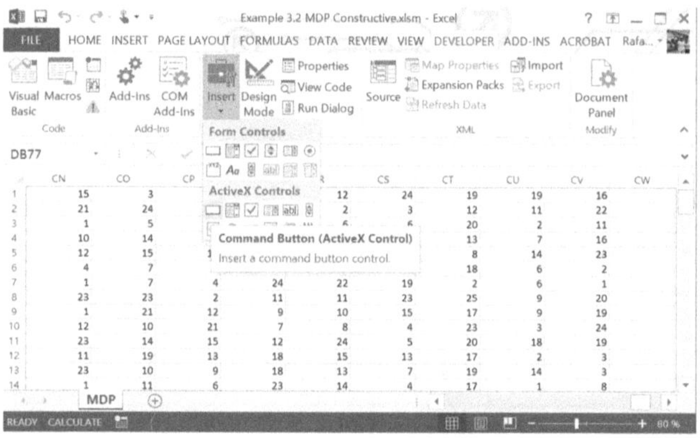

Fig. 3.3 Create a command button

Creating our macro involves two steps. First, create a command button by clicking Insert on the *Developer* tab. Then click the Command Button in the *Activex Controls* group, as shown in Fig. 3.3. The second step is to assign a macro to the command button. To do so, right click *CommandButton1* (make sure *Design Mode* is selected). Next, click *View Code*. The Visual Basic editor appears, and we are ready to start our code! The first and final line of code in our macro are already there: `Private Sub CommandButton1_Click()` and `End sub`, respectively.

When translating an algorithm into code, it is good practice to first define the vectors and variables. In Algorithm 1 above, the elements in the solution are stored in the *M* set. In our code, they are stored in a vector called `Solution`. Figure 3.4

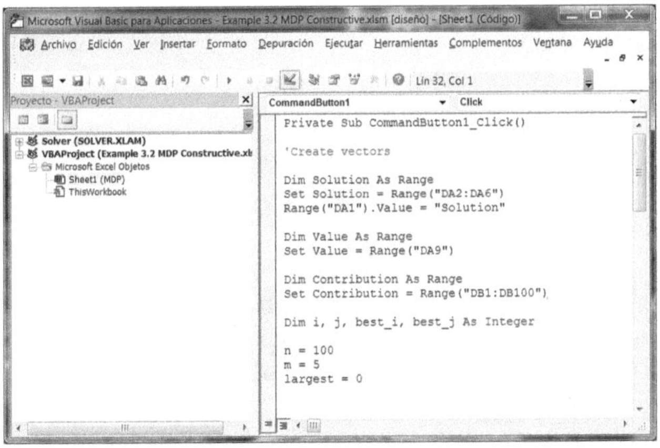

Fig. 3.4 Defining vectors and variables

shows the two corresponding instructions in the code. They use the `Range` function, which specifies the value of a cell or a range of cells in the spreadsheet.

```
Dim Solution As Range
Set Solution = Range("DA2:DA6")
Range("DA1").Value = "Solution"

Dim Value As Range
Set Value = Range("DA9")
Range("DA8").Value = "Value"
```

Using the lines above, we define the `Solution` vector and specify that its five elements are stored in the range `DA2:DA6` of our Excel spreadsheet. The name Solution itself appears in cell `DA1`. Then, in the following lines, we define the `Value` variable in cell `DA9` to store the objective function value of the solution. Its name appears in cell `DA8`. Similarly, we define the contribution vector, called *cont*() in Algorithm 1, and enter the name `Contribution` in the code.

```
Dim Contribution As Range
Set Contribution = Range("DB2:DB101")
Range("DB1").Value = "Contrib."
```

Note that the `Contribution` vector stores a value for each element, so in our problem we need a range with 100 positions. Finally, Fig. 3.4 also shows the `Dim As Integer` instruction, which provides the definition of the variables $i, j, best_i$, and $best_j$ for the following lines of the code. Additionally, some variables are defined in an alternative way, by simply assigning an initial value to them. This is the case with $n = 100, m = 5$, and $largest = 0$.

To compute the two initial elements at the largest distance, called s and t in the description above and `best_i` and `best_j` in the code below, we use two `For` loops nested as follows:

```
For i = 1 To n
For j = 1 To n
  If Cells(i, j).Value > largest Then
    best_i = i
    best_j = j
    largest = Cells(i,j).Value
  End If
Next j
Next i
```

Note that the elements within a loop are slightly indented in the above code. This makes the program more readable. The variable `largest` is updated each time an element in the distance matrix, computed in `Cells(i, j).Value`, is larger than its value. The two associated elements are stored in variables `best_i` and `best_j`, respectively. After the execution of this code, these variables contain the pair of elements with the largest distance, and the solution is initialized as:

```
Solution(1) = best_i
Solution(2) = best_j
Value = largest
```

The first two instructions in the above code initialize the solution with the two elements at the largest distance. The last sentence assigns the largest distance to the `Value` variable. Then, `Contribution(i)` is initialized for each element `i` in the following code, with the sum of the distances from `i` to `best_i` and `best_j`.

```
For i = 1 To n
  Contribution(i)=Cells(i,best_i)+Cells(i,best_j)
Next i
Contribution(best_i)=0
Contribution(best_j)=0
```

Note that in the last two instructions of the above code, the `Contribution` of `best_i` and `best_j` is set to 0 to avoid the selection of these two elements at a later stage of the method.

Once the first two elements have been selected, and the `Contribution` has been initialized, the $m-2$ remaining elements are selected. The following instruction in the code is a `For` loop from 3 to m. Each iteration therefore selects the next element to be added to the partial solution. In particular, the code first identifies the element `best_i` with the largest `Contribution`:

```
largest=0
For i = 1 To n
    If Contribution(i) > largest Then
          largest = Contribution(i)
          best_i = i
    End If
Next i
```

Once the best element is identified, we assign it to the `Solution`, and update its `Value` with:

```
Solution(j) = best_i
Value = Value + largest
```

Note that the largest contribution, computed in the variable `largest` above, provides the number we have to add to the solution value, stored in the `Value` variable, to update it. This is because `largest` is the sum of the distances from `best_i` to the elements in the partial solution under construction, which is exactly the number that we have to add to the solution value. Finally, the `Contribution` of all the elements has to be updated to reflect the inclusion of `best_i` in the solution. This is achieved with the following code:

```
For i = 1 To n
   Contribution(i)=Contribution(i)+Cells(i,best_i)
Next i
Contribution(best_i)=0
```

As mentioned above, all the Visual Basic code explained in this book, can be found in the accompanying Excel files. In particular, this constructive method is implemented in the file *MDP2 Const.xlsm*. As shown in Fig. 3.5, the code is associated with the macro button *Build solution*. If you click on it, you obtain the solution shown in this figure, in which the five selected elements are 1, 55, 4, 62, and 77, with a value of 225. In mathematical terms, we write $M = \{1, 55, 4, 62, 77\}$ and $f(M) = 225$. Note that this solution is better than the one obtained in the previous section with the Evolutionary Solver with a longer CPU time (it had a value of 204).

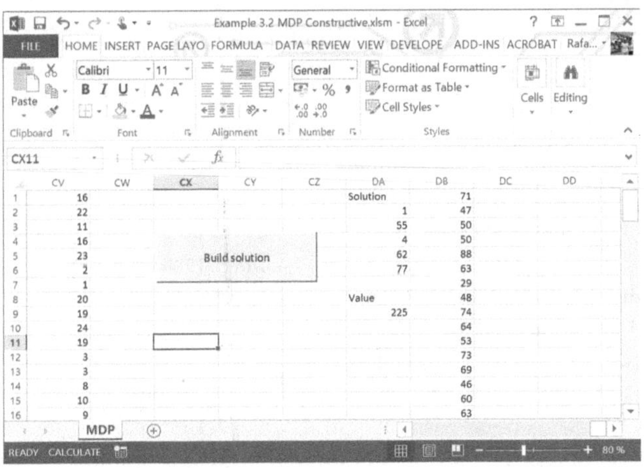

Fig. 3.5 Running the macro

Although this code has already been created in the accompanying file, it is a good exercise to create a new file from scratch, typing it according to the descriptions in this section. In the next section, we explain a more elaborated methodology to obtain improved outcomes.

3.3 The GRASP Methodology

The GRASP methodology was developed in the late 1980s, and this acronym for *greedy randomized adaptive search procedures* was coined in 1995. It was first used in 1989 to solve computationally difficult set covering problems. Each GRASP iteration consists of constructing a trial solution and then applying an improvement procedure to find a local optimum (i.e., the final solution for that iteration). The construction phase is *iterative*, *greedy*, *randomized*, and *adaptive*. It is iterative because the initial solution is built considering one element at a time. It is greedy because the addition of each element is guided by a greedy function. It is randomized because the selection of that element is made in a random fashion. It is adaptive because the element chosen at any iteration in a construction is a function of those chosen previously and relevant information is thus updated from one construction step to the next. The improvement phase typically entails a local search procedure in which the solution is improved, step by step, until no further improvement is possible.

3.3.1 Construction Phase

At each iteration of the construction phase, GRASP maintains a candidate list of elements CL, which can be added to the partial solution under construction, to obtain a feasible complete solution. All candidate elements are evaluated according to a greedy function in order to select the next element to be added. The greedy function usually represents the marginal increase in the cost function by adding the element to the partial solution. Element evaluation is used to create a restricted candidate list RCL with the best elements in CL, i.e., those with the largest incremental contribution in a maximization problem. The element to be added to the partial solution is randomly selected from those in the RCL. Once the selected element is added to the partial solution, the candidate list is updated and the evaluations (incremental contributions) are recalculated.

A particularly appealing characteristic of GRASP is its ease of implementation. We only need to define a construction mechanism according to the above description and a local search procedure. Moreover, the construction usually has one parameter related to the quality of the elements in the RCL. GRASP typically performs a pre-established number of iterations (construction + improvement) and returns the best overall solution.

Based on the greedy constructive method described in the previous section for the Maximum Diversity Problem, we now design a greedy randomized constructive method, according to the GRASP methodology. Given a partial solution M, and a candidate element i to be included in M, its contribution, $cont(i)$, is defined as:

$$cont(i) = \sum_{j \in M} d_{ij}. \tag{3.7}$$

In this constructive method, instead of selecting the element with the largest contribution, which we called a greedy selection, we define a list with the good candidates, and then randomly select an element from this list, which we called a greedy randomized selection.

Algorithm 2: Constructive randomized method

1: Let $G = (V, E)$ be a graph with distance matrix $D = (d_{ij})$
2: $d_{st} \leftarrow \max_{(i,j) \in E} d_{ij}$
3: $M \leftarrow \{s,t\}$ and $f(M) = d_{st}$
4: $CL = V \setminus M$
5: $cont(j) = d_{js} + d_{jt} \ \forall j \in CL$
6: **while** $|M| < m$ **do**
7: $\quad cont_{max} \leftarrow \max_{j \in \mathrm{CL}} cont(j)$
8: $\quad cont_{min} \leftarrow \min_{j \in \mathrm{CL}} cont(j)$
9: $\quad RCL \leftarrow \{j \in CL \mid cont(j) \geq cont_{max} - \alpha \cdot (cont_{max} - cont_{min})\}$
10: $\quad i \leftarrow$ `SelectRandom`(RCL)
11: $\quad M \leftarrow M \cup \{i\}$ and $f(M) = f(M) + cont(i)$
12: $\quad \mathrm{CL} \leftarrow \mathrm{CL} \setminus \{i\}$
13: $\quad cont(i) = 0$
14: $\quad cont(j) = cont(j) + d_{ij} \ \forall j \in CL$
15: **end while**
16: **return** M and $f(M)$

Algorithm 2 shows a pseudo-code of the GRASP construction. We can see that the method is initialized by selecting the two elements, s and t at the largest distance in step 2. This initialization is exactly the same as applied in the greedy construction shown in Algorithm 1. The partial solution set M is initialized with these elements ($M \leftarrow \{s,t\}$ and $f(M) = d_{st}$) in step 3, and the candidate set of elements, CL, which contains all non-selected elements ($CL = V \setminus M$) is created in step 4. The initialization of the method finishes in step 5 , in which the contribution of all the candidate elements is established as the sum of the distances to the two elements in M.

To create the restricted candidate list, RCL, with the good elements that could be added to M, we first calculate the maximum, $cont_{max}$, and the minimum, $cont_{min}$, of the contributions in steps 7 and 8 respectively. Then, we compute RCL as the set of candidate elements with a contribution within a percentage α of this maximum. In mathematical terms:

$$RCL = \{j \in CL \mid cont(j) \geq cont_{max} - \alpha \cdot (cont_{max} - cont_{min})\} \tag{3.8}$$

In step 10 of Algorithm 2, an element i is randomly selected from RCL. Note that if $\alpha = 0$ in Eq. 3.8, RCL only contains the elements with a contribution larger than or equal to the maximum, which means equal to the maximum (since a value cannot be larger than the maximum value). A selection in that RCL is equivalent to a greedy selection of the best candidate. On the other hand, if $\alpha = 1$ in Eq. 3.8, we obtain an RCL with those elements with a contribution larger than or equal to the minimum contribution, which means all the candidate elements (since all of them meet this condition). A selection in that RCL is equivalent to a completely random method, in which we add a randomly selected element to the partial solution. In this way, we can say that $\alpha = 0$ is a greedy method, and $\alpha = 1$ is a random method. Values of α in [0,1] would therefore reflect a combination of greediness and randomization.

The *While* loop in Algorithm 2 takes place from steps 6 to 15, reflecting the successive applications of this part of the code. In each one, the RCL is created, an element $i \in RCL$ is randomly selected, and the different elements of the algorithm are updated. In particular, in step 11, i is included in M and its value updated ($f(M) = f(M) + cont(i)$), and in step 12, it is removed from CL. Finally, the contribution value of all the non-selected elements is increased in step 14 by adding their distance to i. Note that to prevent the selection of already selected elements, we set the contribution of i to 0 in step 13. The method finishes when the while loop performs $m - 2$ iterations (i.e., when $|M| = m$). In the next subsection, we can see how to implement this method in Visual Basic for Excel. The file *MDP3 GRASP Const.xlsm* contains this code.

3.3.2 *The Visual Basic Macro*

To create the code of our GRASP constructive method, we are going to edit the code of the greedy constructive method shown in Sect. 3.2.1, adding new elements, and replacing others.

In the first part of the code, where the declaration of the vectors is, we insert the restricted candidate list, RCL, definition as:

```
Dim RCL As Range
Set RCL = Range("DC2:DC100")
Range("DC1").Value = "RCL"
```

We can see in the code above that, since we do not know the size of RCL, we simply give it a maximum dimension of 100 (considering that eventually all the elements could be in RCL). We create it in column DC of our Excel file. We also insert in the variable definitions, the initializations of the following three variables related to RCL:

```
Dim rcl_elements As Integer
Dim rcl_th As Double
rcl_alpha=0.8
```

The fist variable defined above, `rcl_elements`, counts the number of elements in RCL. The second variable, `rcl_th` stores the value of the threshold for the RCL inclusion. It is computed from the `rcl_alpha`, which sets the value of the so called α parameter described in the previous subsection. We set this latter parameter to 0.8, but other values in [0,1] could lead to better solutions. The only way to know it, is to try with the different values on different data instances.

The initialization of the method is the same here than in the pure greedy code in Sect. 3.2.1. It basically finds the two elements at the largest distance and include them in the solution. Then, we perform $m-2$ iterations with a `For` loop, to add elements, one by one, to the solution. There, we first identify the element `Best_i` with the largest contribution, and then add it to the solution. Now, we also identify `Best_i`, but instead of adding it to the solution, we build the RCL with this code:

```
rcl_th = largest * rcl_alpha
rcl_elements = 0
For i = 1 To n
   If Contribution(i) > rcl_th Then
      rcl_elements = rcl_elements + 1
      RCL(rcl_elements) = i
   End If
Next i
k = Int(rcl_elements * Rnd()) + 1
best_i = RCL(k)
```

In the first line of the code above, we set the threshold `rcl_th` as a fraction of the `largest` value. Note that we are not using the standard definition of RCL shown in the expression (3.8), but we are considering here a simplified approach. There are different ways to compute a restricted candidate list, and this is a simple one in which we only perform one operation to compute the threshold. The `For` loop above, checks, for each element `i`, its possible inclusion in RCL, by comparing its contribution, `Contribution(i)`, with the threshold `rcl_th`. The variable `rcl_elements` is incremented by one unit each time an element is added to RCL. Once all the elements have been scanned, in the last two lines, an index `k`, is randomly selected in the range $[1, rcl\_elements]$, and the associated element in RCL, `RCL(k)`, assigned to the `best_i` variable. In this way, we can directly apply the rest of the code introduced in the greedy construction, in which the selected element, `best_i`, is added to the partial solution, and the algorithm elements are updated accordingly. Section 3.5 shows the entire code of this greedy randomized constructive method.

Performing multiple GRASP iterations may be interpreted as a means of strategically sampling the solution space. Based on empirical observations, it has been found that the sampling distribution generally has a mean value that is inferior to the one obtained by a deterministic construction, but the best over all trials dominates the deterministic solution with a high probability. The intuitive justification of this phenomenon is based on the ordering statistics of sampling. Figure 3.6 illustrates this point. It shows an histogram created from the objective function values of 1000 solutions obtained with the GRASP construction phase described in this section.

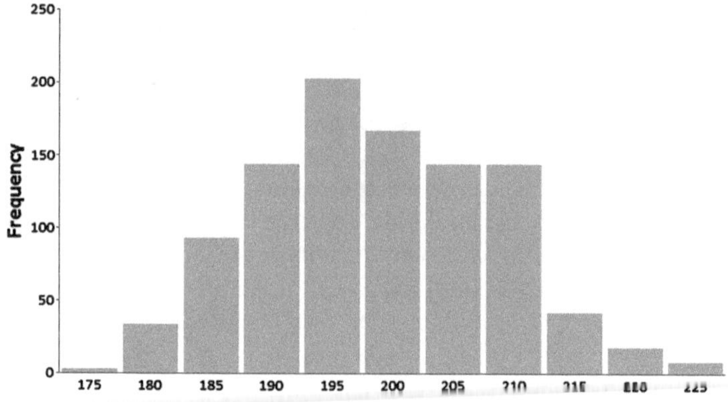

Fig. 3.6 Solution value of multiple GRASP constructions

The histogram in Fig. 3.6 shows that the objective function values of the 1,000 solutions generated with the GRASP constructive method range from 175 to values slightly larger than 230. The first class depicted in this diagram collects the few values obtained in the range from 175 to 180. Note that Excel labels this class with 175. A relative large number of solutions exhibit a value larger than 204, which corresponds to the value of the greedy (deterministic) solution obtained in the previous section.

3.3.3 Local Search Phase

The second stage of a GRASP algorithm consists of improving the constructed solutions using a local search method, which will guide the search process to a local optimum. Local search methods are based on the notion of neighbor structures that generate changes to move from one solution to another in the solution space. Local searches perform moves as long as the current solution improves and terminate when no further improvement is possible. The resulting solution is said to be locally optimal (i.e., the solution cannot be improved within the defined neighbor structure).

A local search is based on performing consecutive improving moves until no further improvement is possible. In this way, from an initial solution, it visits some intermediate solutions, until the final one, the local optimum, is reached. It is sometimes called a trajectory based method, since this succession of solutions describes a trajectory in the solution space. It is important to remark that local search strongly depends on the move definition, for which different alternatives can be considered. The most popular are exchanges and insertions. In the Maximum Diversity Problem, given that the number of elements in the solution must be m, exchanges are the natural approach. Anyway, the move definition must consists of a small change in the solution, which permits a fast evaluation of the resulting solution. In this way, the method can perform many moves within a short computational time. The set of solutions that can be reached applying a move to the current solution is called *the neighborhood*.

One of the key elements in designing an effective local search method is the definition of the *move* and the associated *move value* (change in the objective function value). In particular, for the MDP we define $\texttt{move}(M,i,j)$ as the move that interchanges vertex $i \in M$ with vertex $j \in V \setminus M$. This move usually produces a variation in the objective function, denoted as $\texttt{move\_value}(M,i,j)$. If the move value is positive, it indicates that in a maximization problem, such as the MDP, the associated move improves the solution. We therefore would apply the move and obtain a new solution better than M.

Given a solution M, an element $i \in M$, and an element $j \in V \setminus M$, the move value can be computed as follows. If i is removed from the solution, its value would decrease in the sum of the distances from i to the rest of the elements in M. In mathematical terms,

$$out\_value(i) = \sum_{u \in M} d_{ui}. \tag{3.9}$$

On the other hand, if j is added to the solution, its value would increase in the sum of the distances from j to the elements in M (excluding the i). In mathematical terms,

$$in\_value(j) = \sum_{u \in M, u \neq i} d_{uj}. \tag{3.10}$$

Then, the move value can be computed from these two values as:

$$move\_value(M,i,j) = in\_value(j) - out\_value(i) \tag{3.11}$$

The local search method scans, at each iteration, the list of elements in the solution ($i \in M$) in lexicographical order (i.e., from the first to the last one). Algorithm 3 shows a *for* statement in line 3, in which the index i takes values from 1 to m to examine M in a loop. Then, for each element, $i \in M$, it examines the list of unselected elements ($j \in V \setminus M$) in search for the first improving exchange (i.e., $move\_value(M,i,j) > 0$). The unselected elements are also examined in lexicographical order (from 1 to n) in line 6 of Algorithm 3. The method performs the first improving move ($M \leftarrow M \setminus \{i\} \cup \{j\}$) in line 10. It then updates the objective function value $f(M)$ in line 11, by adding the move value to it. This concludes the current iteration in the inner *while* loop (lines 9 to 18). The algorithm repeats iterations as long as improving moves can be performed, and stops when no further improvement is possible. Note that when an improving move is performed, the i index is reset to 0 in line 13, and then the *for* loop is initiated again in 1 (the *end for* statement in line 16 increments i in one unit, and thus it takes the value 1). In this way, the method only terminates when all the elements in the solution have been examined an no move has been performed. We can then assure that the current solution is a local optimum.

Algorithm 3: Local search method

```
Let M be a solution with m elements, and f(M) its value
CL = V \ M
for i=1 to m do
    Compute out_value(i)
    Move=0
    while Move = 0 and CL not explored do
        j ← SelectNext(CL)
        Compute in_value(j)
        if in_value(j) > out_value(i) then
            M ← M \ {i} ∪ {j}
            f(M) ← f(M) + in_value(j) − out_value(i)
            CL ← CL \ {j} ∪ {i}
            Move = 1 and i = 0
        end if
    end while
end for
return M and f(M)
```

3.3.4 *The Visual Basic Macro*

An efficient implementation of the local search has to check very fast whether an element is or not in the solution, in order to evaluate the moves. We therefore create a binary vector, called `InSol`, in which `InSol(i)` takes the value 1 if the element `i` is in the solution, and 0 otherwise.

We start our macro by defining the following three elements: `Solution, Value` and `InSol`. The first two were already used in the construction. The third one goes from cell 2 to 101 in column `DD` with the text *Is in Sol?* in the first row indicating its content.

```
Dim Solution As Range
Set Solution = Range("DA2:DA6")

Dim Value As Range
Set Value = Range("DA9")

Dim InSol As Range
Set InSol = Range("DD2:DD101")
InSol.Value = 0
Range("DD1").Value = "Is in Sol?"
```

To complete the initialization of the method, we define the variables. Special mention deserve `try_out`, which records the candidate element in the solution to be removed from it, and `try_in`, which records the element not in the solution that we are considering to add to it. The following code summarizes the initialization, in which we basically put a 1 in the positions of `InSol` corresponding to elements in the solution.

```
Dim i, j, try_out, try_in, element As Integer
Dim Move, out_value, in_value As Integer

n = 100
m = 5

For i = 1 To m
    element = Solution(i).Value
    InSol(element) = 1
Next i
```

As can be seen in Sect. 3.5, the main part of the local search code is in the outer `For` loop, in which the elements in `Solution` are examined one by one. Specifically, the index `i` goes from 1 to `n`, and at each iteration, the element `Solution(i)` is considered to be removed from the solution. To do that, it is assigned to the `try_out` variable in the statement `try_out=Solution(i)`. Then, the `out_value` described in the previous section is computed in the following code:

```
out_value = 0
For j = 1 To m
    element = Solution(j)
    out_value=out_value+Cells(try_out,element).Value
Next j
```

The code above computes the `out_value` variable, which is initialized to 0 in the first line. For each `element` in the solution, this code adds to `out_value` its distance to the `try_out` element. In this way, after all the elements in the solution have been considered, the variable contains the sum of the distances from `try_out` to the rest of elements.

In the next loop we scan the candidate elements to be included in the solution when `try_out` is removed from it. We are computing the `in_value` for any `try_in` element. As soon as an improvement move is found, the move is performed (i.e., when `in_value>out_value` for a `try_in` element). This is why instead a `For` loop, we use now a `While` loop that permits to abandon it if an additional condition is met. Specifically, we define the `Move` variable initialized with a 0. Note that the `While` loop iterates as long as this variable remains equal to 0 (and `try_in` is lower than or equal to the number of elements `n`). If we find an improvement move, we change this variable to 1, which forces to quit the loop. If we don't find an improvement move, but the `n` elements have been explored, the loop also finishes.

```
Move = 0
try_in = 1
While Move = 0 And try_in <= n
   in_value = 0
   If InSol(try_in)=0 Then
        For j = 1 To m
           element = Solution(j)
           If element <> try_out Then
              in_value=in_value+Cells(try_in,element).Value
```

```
            End If
        Next j
    End If
```

Note that in the code above, we check two important items. The first one is that the `try_in` element is not in the solution. This is done in the statement `If InSol(try_in)=0`. The second is that to compute the `in_value` we sum all the distances from `try_in` to the elements in the solution, with the exception to the `try_out`, since it will not be part of the solution after being removed. We check that we are not adding this distance with the statement `If element<>try_out`. Note that in Visual Basic the <> symbol stands for *not equal to*.

The While loop in the code above is unfinished. It is completed with the code below, in which we check in the first line if the exchange of elements improves the solution. In this case, `try_in` is added to the solution, and the `Value` and `InSol` are updated.

```
    If in_value > out_value Then
        Solution(i) = try_in
        Value = Value - out_value + in_value
        InSol(try_out) = 0
        InSol(try_in) = 1
        Move = 1
        i = 0
    End If

    try_in=try_in+1
Wend
```

The `While` loop above finishes, after increasing `try_in` by one unit, with the `Wend` instruction. The program execution then returns to the `While` instruction. If the two conditions are satisfied, `Move=0` and `try_in<=n`, the loop is performed again with the new `try_in` value. In other words, in this loop we explore the `try_in` elements not present in the solution, until all of them have been explored, or until we find one `try_in` element to exchange with `try_out`, producing an improved solution.

The logical structure of the local search code basically consists of two loops. The outer `For` loop, in which a `try_out` element is considered for removal, and the inner `While` loop, in which a `try_in` element is considered for insertion. When both loops finished, we have explored the elements in the solution, and eventually performed some improvement moves. Note, however, that the final solution could be further improved. When a move is made, the solution changes, and we have to explore all the elements in the solution again before stopping the search. This is why, in the code above, if a move is performed, we set the `i` variable to 1 within the `If` condition, initiating the exploration of the solution again. In this way, when both loops finished, we can assure that the final solution cannot be further improved with exchanges. In other words, the output of the local search is a local optimum.

Once the code is implemented, as in the file *MDP4 GRASP.xlsm*, we can easily obtain a solution by simply clicking on the associated *activex button*. If we click on the GRASP construction button, we will obtain a relatively good initial solution. For example $M = \{1, 55, 18, 85, 62\}$, which has a value of 174. Then, if we click the local search button, we improve it, obtaining the local optimum $M = \{65, 51, 99, 54, 62\}$ with a value of 232. Note that the randomization makes that we obtain different solutions in each computer. If we repeat this combination (construction + improvement) several times, we will easily obtain even better solutions than this one, such as the $M = \{88, 38, 6, 20, 25\}$ with a value of 235. Note however, that although this solution is very good, better than any other previously mentioned, we cannot say that it is the optimal solution. As a mater of fact, with a heuristic method, such as GRASP, we do not know how far the solution obtained is from the optimum.

3.4 Reactive GRASP

Our code in the previous sections allows us to easily test different values of the α parameter and see the associated results for a given instance. However, if we repeat the comparison in a different instance, a different value of α might now perform better. This is why to be able to reach a significant conclusion, we have to perform our experiments in a large set of instances and compute the average value of the solutions obtained. This enables us to compare different parameter values, or in general, variants of the method.

A different approach is Reactive GRASP. Here, the value of the parameter is randomly determined for each instance according to an empirical distribution of probabilities. We limit this section to the theoretical description and we are not going to show how to do this in Excel. This is advanced material that is included for those that want to create more powerful methods.

During the initial constructions of the reactive method, the value of α is randomly selected from the set $S = \{0, 0.1, 0.2, \ldots 0.9, 1\}$ with a uniform distribution. 20% of the constructions sample from the uniform distribution, while 80% sample according to the *hits* value. In each iteration, we test whether the constructed solution $x(a)$ obtained with $\alpha = a$ has a value $z(x(a))$ within a pre-established threshold of the best constructed solution so far. We have empirically found that a conservative value of 90% for this threshold provides good results. In this case, we increment $hits(a)$ by one unit (where $hits(i)$ is initially set to zero for all $i \in S$). Otherwise, $hits(a)$ remains unchanged. Therefore, all the values considered in S initially have the same possibility of being selected for construction. However, as the algorithm progresses, those values better suited for a particular instance (those that produce better constructions) are more frequently selected. In this way, the reactive construction customizes the best value (or values) of the parameter for each instance. Note that in the non-reactive variants described earlier, the parameter is selected offline and adjusted to a fixed value for all the instances considered.

We now compare three non-reactive GRASP constructions with the reactive variant described above. In particular, we consider the Max-Min Diversity Problem, and a set of 40 instances formed with 20 instances with $n = 100$ and 20 with $n = 25$ (half with $m = 0.1n$ and half with $m = 0.3n$). For each GRASP variant and instance pair we obtain 100 solutions, and consider several statistics to evaluate its performance.

In each experiment, we compute for each instance the overall best solution value, *BestValue*, obtained by all executions of the methods considered. Then, for each method, we compute the relative percentage deviation between the best solution value obtained with that method and *BestValue* for that instance. We report the average of this relative percentage deviation (Dev.) across all the instances considered in each particular experiment. Finally, for each method, we report the number of instances (#Best) in which the value of the best solution obtained with this method matches *BestValue*. We also report the statistic *Score* achieved by each method. For each instance, the *n_score* of a method M is defined as the number of methods that found a better solution than M. In case of ties, all the methods receive the same *n_score*, equal to the number of methods strictly better than all of them. We then report Score as the sum of the *n_score* values across all the instances in the experiment. Thus, the lower the Score the better the method. Table 3.3 reports, for this set of 40 instances and each value of α, the values of Dev., #Best, and Score described above.

Table 3.3 Comparison of GRASP variants

	$\alpha = 0.75$	$\alpha = 0.90$	$\alpha = 0.95$	Reactive
Dev.	9.23%	2.51%	1.09%	0.81%
#Best	0	5	10	16
Score	277	184	101	60

The results in Table 3.3 show that the best outcomes are obtained when the constructive method is run with the reactive strategy, since this results in the lowest average deviation and the largest number of best solutions.

3.5 Exercises

1. In the GRASP construction described in Sect. 3.3.1 the restricted candidate list RCL is computed using the minimum and maximum of the candidate elements evaluation. Equation 3.8 provides the mathematical expression. However, the code in Sect. 3.3.2 does not apply this expression, and implements a simplified version based only in the maximum evaluation. Implement now the RCL according to the Eq. 3.8.

2. The following code generates a matrix with n rows and n columns with random elements in the range $[0, 25]$. Apply it to generate a MDP instance with 250 rows and 250 columns. Adapt the GRASP Visual Basic code described in Sect. 3.5 to target this instance.

```
For i = 1 To n
  Cells(i, i).Value = 0
  For j = i + 1 To n
     Cells(i, j).Value = Int(25 * Rnd()) + 1
     Cells(j, i).Value = Cells(i, j).Value
  Next j
Next i
```

3. The local search method described in Sect. 3.3.3 and its associated Visual Basic code in Sect. 3.3.4 implement a *first-improvement* strategy (also known as *mildest ascent*). At each iteration, the method scans the neighborhood of a solution and performs the first improving move found. In other words, it stops the neighborhood search as soon as an improving switch (move) is identified. An alternative is the so-called *best-improvement* strategy. In this strategy, solutions are improved by performing a sequence of steps that are based on examining the entire neighborhood of the current solution and selecting the best move to make. The neighborhood in our Maximum Diversity Problem, consists of all possible switches (or exchanges) of an element in the solution ($i \in M$), with an element not in the solution ($j \in CL$). The entire neighborhood is calculated at each step and the switch that produces the largest improvement to the objective function value is selected. To implement this strategy, if we consider the pseudo-code in algorithm 3, instead of using the *Move* variable and the *While* loop in step 6, we have to use a *For* loop to examine all the *j*-candidates to exchange with an element *i*. Implement this strategy, and compare its result with those of the first strategy on an MDP example.

4. The procedure described in Sect. 3.3.1 implements a typical GRASP construction where each candidate element is first evaluated by a greedy function to construct the *RCL*, and an element is then randomly selected from the *RCL*. We now consider an alternative construction procedure first applying the random component and then the greedy selection. Create a new constructive method for the MDP, called GRC2, in which we first choose candidates completely at random, and then evaluate each candidate according to a greedy function to make the greedy choice. GRC2 first constructs the restricted candidate list *RCL2* with a fraction β ($0 \leq \beta \leq 1$) of the elements in *CL* selected at random. Then, it evaluates all the elements in *RCL2*, computing its contribution, and selects the best one. Create the Visual Basic code of GRC2 and report the value obtained with this method in the instance in the Excel file *MDP1.xlsx*.

5. The file *MDP3 GRASP Const.xlsm* contains the Visual Basic code of a standard GRASP construction for the MDP. The α parameter is set to 0.8 in that code. Edit it, to transform that implementation into a Reactive GRASP, in which the α parameter is determined during the run according to the description in Sect. 3.4.

6. The procedures described in this chapter, solve the Max-Sum Diversity Problem. We now consider the Max-Min Diversity Problem, in which we select a

set M of m elements from V, for which the minimum distance between its elements is maximum. In this exercise we consider a GRASP construction for the Min-Max version. In particular, the construction procedure GRC performs m steps to produce a solution with m elements. At each step, GRC selects a candidate element $i^* \in CL = V \setminus M$ with a large distance to the elements in the partial solution M. Specifically, it first computes d_j as the minimum distance between element j and the selected elements. Then, it constructs the restricted candidate list RCL with all the candidate (unselected) elements j with a distance value d_j within a fraction α $(0 \leq \alpha \leq 1)$ of the maximum distance $d^* = \max\{d_j \mid j \in CL\}$. Finally, GRC randomly selects an element in RCL.

7. In Chaps. 1 and 2 we discuss solution representations and search spaces. In this chapter we solve the MDP with a heuristic method based on a solution with 100 binary variables. Consider now a solution represented with 5 variables, with the index of the chosen elements. Apply the GRASP methodology to create a heuristic method to solve this problem.

Appendix: Visual Basic Code

In this appendix we simply put together the code introduced in Sects. 3.3.2 and 3.3.4. In this way, the reader can type it to create a macro in the Excel file. As mentioned above, all the code introduced here is already in the accompanying Excel file. However, we believe that it is a good exercise to type it and see, line by line, how it works.

GRASP construction Code

```
'CREATE DATA STRUCTURES
Dim Solution As Range
Set Solution = Range("DA2:DA6")
Range("DA1").Value = "Solution"

Dim Value As Range
Set Value = Range("DA9")
Range("DA8").Value = "Value"

Dim Contribution As Range
Set Contribution = Range("DB2:DB101")
Range("DB1").Value = "Contrib."

Dim RCL As Range
Set RCL = Range("DC2:DC100")
Range("DC1").Value = "RCL"

Dim i, j, best_i, best_j As Integer
Dim rcl_elements As Integer
```

```
Dim rcl_th As Double

'PROBLEM DIMENSION AND PARAMETERS
n = 100
m = 5
largest = 0
rcl_alpha = 0.8

'FIND THE 2 INITIAL ELEMENTS
For i = 1 To n
For j = 1 To n

    If Cells(i, j).Value > largest Then
        best_i = i
        best_j = j
        largest = Cells(i, j).Value
    End If

Next j
Next i

'ADD THE ELEMENTS TO THE SOLUTION
Solution(1) = best_i
Solution(2) = best_j
Value = largest

'INITIALIZE CONTRIBUTIONS
For i = 1 To n
Contribution(i) = Cells(i, best_i) + Cells(i, best_j)
Next i
Contribution(best_i) = 0
Contribution(best_j) = 0

'SELECT THE REST OF THE ELEMENTS
For j = 3 To m
    largest = 0
    For i = 1 To n
        If Contribution(i) > largest Then
            largest = Contribution(i)
            best_i = i
        End If
    Next i

    'CREATE THE RCL
    rcl_th = largest * rcl_alpha
    rcl_elements = 0

    For i = 1 To n
        If Contribution(i) > rcl_th Then
            rcl_elements = rcl_elements + 1
            RCL(rcl_elements) = i
        End If
    Next i
```

```
    'SELECT AN ELEMENT AT RANDOM IN RCL
    k = Int(rcl_elements * Rnd()) + 1
    best_i = RCL(k)

    'ADD THE ELEMENT TO THE SOLUTION
    Solution(j) = best_i
    Value = Value + Contribution(best_i)

    'UPDATE THE CONTRIBUTION
    For i = 1 To n
        Contribution(i) = Contribution(i) + Cells(i, best_i)
    Next i
    Contribution(best_i) = 0

Next j
```

GRASP Local Search Code

```
'CREATE DATA STRUCTURES
Dim Solution As Range
Set Solution = Range("DA2:DA6")

Dim Value As Range
Set Value = Range("DA9")

Dim InSol As Range
Set InSol = Range("DD2:DD101")
InSol.Value = 0
Range("DD1").Value = "Is in Sol?"

Dim i, j, try_out, try_in, element As Integer
Dim Move, out_value, in_value As Integer

'PROBLEM DIMENSION
n = 100
m = 5

'INITIALIZE ARRAY INSOL
For i = 1 To m
    element = Solution(i).Value
    InSol(element) = 1
Next i

'TRY TO REPLACE EVERY ELEMENT IN THE SOLUTION
For i = 1 To m
    try_out = Solution(i)

    out_value = 0
    For j = 1 To m
        element = Solution(j)
```

```
        out_value = out_value + Cells(try_out, element).Value
    Next j

    Move = 0
    try_in = 1
    While Move = 0 And try_in <= n

        'COMPUTE THE IN_VALUE OF TRY_IN
        in_value = 0
        If InSol(try_in) = 0 Then
            For j = 1 To m
                element = Solution(j)
                If element <> try_out Then
                    in_value = in_value + Cells(try_in, element).Value
                End If
            Next j
        End If

        ' PERFORM THE MOVE
        If in_value > out_value Then
            Solution(i) = try_in
            Value = Value - out_value + in_value
            InSol(try_out) = 0
            InSol(try_in) = 1
            Move = 1
            i = 0
        End If

        try_in = try_in + 1
    Wend
Next i
```

References

1. Duarte, A., and R. Martí. 2007. Tabu search and GRASP for the maximum diversity problem. *European Journal of Operational Research* 178: 7184.
2. Feo, T.A., and M.G.C. Resende. 1989. A probabilistic heuristic for a computationally difficult set covering problem. *Operations Research Letters* 8: 6771.
3. Feo, T.A., and M.G.C. Resende. 1995. Greedy randomized adaptive search procedures. *Journal of Global Optimization* 6: 109133.
4. Kiong, L.V. 2010. *Excel VBA made easy: A concise guide for beginners*. Paramount CA: Createspace.
5. Martí, R., M. Gallego, A. Duarte, and E.G. Pardo. 2013. Heuristics and metaheuristics for the maximum diversity problem. *Journal of Heuristics* 19 (4): 591–615.
6. Prokopyev, O.A., N. Kong, and D.L. Martinez-Torres. 2009. The equitable dispersion problem. *European Journal of Operational Research* 197: 59–67.
7. Resende, M.G.C., and C.C. Ribeiro. 2014. GRASP: Greedy randomized adaptive search procedures. In *Search methodologies*, eds. Burke, E.K., Kendall, G, 287–312. US: Springer

Chapter 4
Tabu Search

4.1 Introduction

In this chapter we describe one of the most successful methodologies for obtaining high quality solutions to difficult optimization problems. It was proposed by Fred Glover [3] under the term Tabu Search, which refers to the way in which the method explores the solution region of a given problem. We will use Clustering Analysis as an example to apply this technique.

Clustering analysis is an analytic tool to identify groups in data. This identification usually has the objective of finding underlying patterns. A cluster is a group of elements or objects that belong to the same class. In other words, similar objects are grouped in one cluster, and dissimilar objects are grouped in different clusters. An interesting application of clustering analysis can be found in the context of *market segmentation*, in which companies want to segment customers to apply unique treatment to each segment. This area has received much attention in the last years, and is a cornerstone in business analytics.

The clustering process begins with deciding which variables to use for grouping or classification. Many attributes may be associated with objects in a study but feature selection techniques are often applied to reduce the number to be used for cluster analysis. The type of variables can provide different segments or groups, and sometimes their choice is apparent because of the context or the problem being study. In other cases however, we have to choose them considering that they are able to differentiate segments. From a statistical point of view, we have to avoid the use of highly correlated variables since they would cover the same information.

Once we have selected the variables, we must have a way to measure the similarity between a pair of objects. Most clustering methods are based on a distance function, which measures the (dis)similarity between pairs of objects. The *Euclidean distance* is probably the most popular. Two objects, A and B, with two attributes each one, can be represented as $A = (x_A, y_A)$ and $B = (x_B, y_B)$. The Euclidean distance between A and B, simply denoted $d(A, B)$, is computed as:

A. Duarte et al., *Metaheuristics for Business Analytics*, EURO Advanced Tutorials on Operational Research, https://doi.org/10.1007/978-3-319-68119-1_4

$$d(A,B) = \sqrt{(x_A - x_B)^2 + (y_A - y_B)^2}. \tag{4.1}$$

Alternative distance measures are: The *Manhattan distance*, which computes the sum of the absolute differences of the attributes, and the *Chebychev distance*, which computes the maximum of the absolute differences of the attributes. We will consider the Euclidean distance in our examples, since it is the most widely used. While feature selection is a dimensionality reduction technique, cluster analysis (or clustering) is a data-reduction technique because it allows to address groups instead of individual observations.

Example 4.1. Consider a small department in a university with 15 professors, where the authorities want to identify different groups or clusters to apply specific policies and actions in each group. The performance of each faculty member is evaluated in terms of both teaching and research, and we want to use these two values (variables) to classify or group the professors in this department. The teaching value is computed in the range [0, 7] from a survey to the students, which reflect their opinion on the instructors. On the other hand, the research evaluation is a normalized value, in the range [0, 10], computing the number of scientific papers published in the last five years. The file *Cluster1 Data.xlsm* contains these two values for the 15 professors in the department, as well as their pairwise Euclidean distances computed from these two variables.

From the evaluation in Table 4.1 (Teaching, Research), depicted in Fig. 4.1, we can easily compute the distance between a pair of professors. For example, the distance between R.M. (Id. 1) and J.P. (Id. 2) is 3.66, as computed with the expression:

$$d(1,2) = \sqrt{(2.9-5)^2 + (6-3)^2} = \sqrt{(-2.1)^2 + 3^2} = 3.66. \tag{4.2}$$

With the expression above we compute all the pairwise distances collected in file *Cluster1 Data.xlsm*. From this distance matrix we can apply a clustering algorithm to identify groups or clusters in this set of professors. In this way, we can establish which professors are similar in terms of teaching and or research, and which are different.

4.2 Classic Clustering Methods

We now describe a clustering method, i.e., a method which follows a given principle for creating groups from the data. There are many clustering procedures, being *agglomerative clustering* one of the most popular. In this method, groups are con-

Table 4.1 Performance evaluation

Prof. Id.	Name	Teaching	Research
1	R.M.	2.9	6
2	J.P.	5	3
3	M.L.	3	6.5
4	A.C.	1.5	2
5	R.T.	1.4	3.5
6	D.F.	5	7
7	E.J.	5.7	2.3
8	S.P.	2	4.2
9	R.F.	5.9	7
10	E.A.	6	7.2
11	T.Y.	5	9.3
12	S.L.	3.2	8
13	A.P.	5.4	4
14	E.Y.	3.8	7.1
15	R.Y.	2.8	7

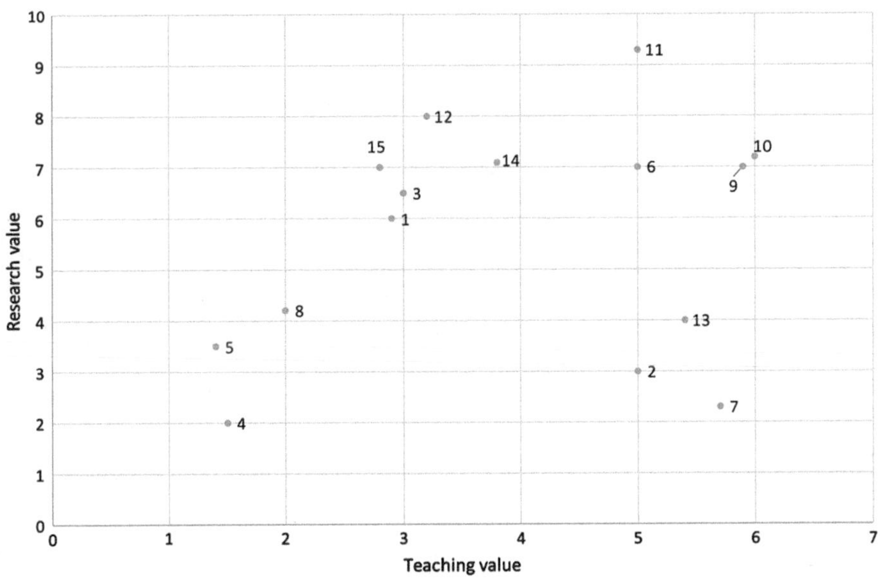

Fig. 4.1 Problem data

secutively formed from individuals or, in general objects. This iterative procedure starts by considering that each element or object is in an individual cluster. Then, clusters are iteratively merged, grouping two of them into a single one in each step.

Therefore, the number of clusters is reduced by one unit in each step. The method finishes when the desired number of clusters is reached.

We can find in the business analytics literature several agglomerative procedures that follow the method described above. The main difference between them can be found in the definition of the distance between a newly formed cluster to an object, or to other clusters. There are five classic methods, depending on the definition of the distance between two clusters. They are:

- *Closest neighbor* (single linkage). The distance between two clusters is the minimum or shortest distance between any two objects in the two clusters (i.e., the minimum distance of all the pairs with one element in a cluster and the other element in the other cluster).
- *Furthest neighbor* (complete linkage). The distance between two clusters is the maximum or the largest distance between any two objects in the two clusters.
- *Centroid.* The distance between two clusters is computed from the geometric center (called centroid) of each cluster. Specifically, it is computed as the distance between their centroids.
- *Average linkage.* This is a variant of the first two methods in which the distance between clusters is computed as the average distance between their elements.
- *Median linkage.* Similarly to the previous one, in this method the distance between clusters is computed as the median of the distances between their elements.

Another family of clustering procedures is given by the so-called partitioning methods, being the *k-means* the most important in this group. It follows a different principle than the agglomerative methods above. Specifically, the procedure partitions the data minimizing the within-cluster variation (the distance from each object to the center of its cluster). Starting from a random assignment of objects to clusters, the k-means method successively reassigns objects to other clusters as long as the within-cluster variation is reduced.

We apply the single linkage method to the data in the Example 4.1, stopping when we obtain four clusters. Figure 4.2 shows the four groups in a geometric representation. We can see that in a first cluster, we have $C_1 = \{4,5,8\}$. This cluster contains those professors with a low teaching and research rating. In the opposite extreme, we can find another cluster, $C_2 = \{6,9,10,11\}$ with those with very good teaching and research values. Between these two groups, we can identify the other two groups depicted in Fig. 4.2. Cluster $C_3 = \{2,7,13\}$, which contains professors with a low research value, but with a relative good teaching value, and symmetrically, Cluster $C_4 = \{1,3,12,14,15\}$ contains professors with low teaching value and good research value. It is clear that this information is very useful to the authorities of the university to know the status of the faculty and to create rules and policies to improve their performance.

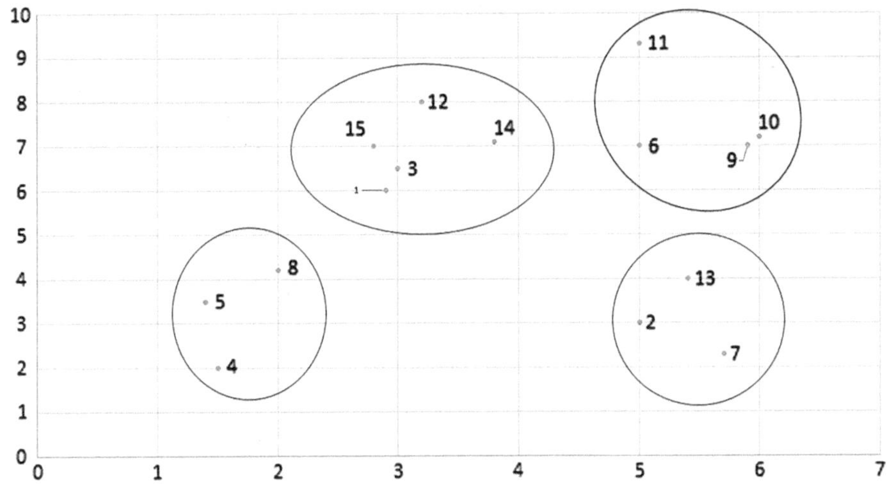

Fig. 4.2 Clusters in Example 4.1

4.3 A Clustering Method Based on Optimization

From a mathematical point of view, we can see that clustering seeks groups with a small intra-group distance and large inter-group distance.

It must be noted that the example considered in Sect. 4.2 is very small and that the elements are arranged in a way that it is very easy to identify the four groups encountered. The four groups can be identified by simply glancing at the diagram in Fig. 4.1. However, visual inspection is not a viable clustering method when the data set has many dimensions and observations. As a matter of fact, clustering can be a very difficult problem and the classic methods may perform poorly in many instances.

An interesting approach to the clustering problem is to define it as an optimization problem. There are many different ways to address it, we consider in this section a simple formulation in which the number of clusters is established beforehand.

Clustering problems can be formulated as quadratic integer programs with binary variables x_{ig} that take the value of 1 if element i is in group g and 0 otherwise. A quadratic integer programming formulation of a clustering problem in which we want to group n elements in k clusters is:

$$\min \quad \textstyle\sum_{g=1}^{k} \sum_{i=1}^{n-1} \sum_{j>1}^{n} d_{ij} x_{ig} x_{jg} \tag{4.3}$$

$$\textstyle\sum_{g=1}^{k} x_{ig} = 1, 1 \leq i \leq n \tag{4.4}$$

$$\textstyle\sum_{i=1}^{n} x_{ig} \geq 1, 1 \leq g \leq k \tag{4.5}$$

$$x_{ig} \in \{0, 1\}, 1 \leq i \leq n, 1 \leq g \leq k. \tag{4.6}$$

The objective function adds the distance of all pairs of elements that belong to the same group. The first set of constraints forces the assignment of each element to a group. The second set of constraints forces the size of all groups to be larger than or equal to 1. We can easily implement this model in Excel, as shown in the accompanying file *Cluster2 MathModel.xlsm*, to solve Example 4.1. Fig. 4.3 shows the spreadsheet design.

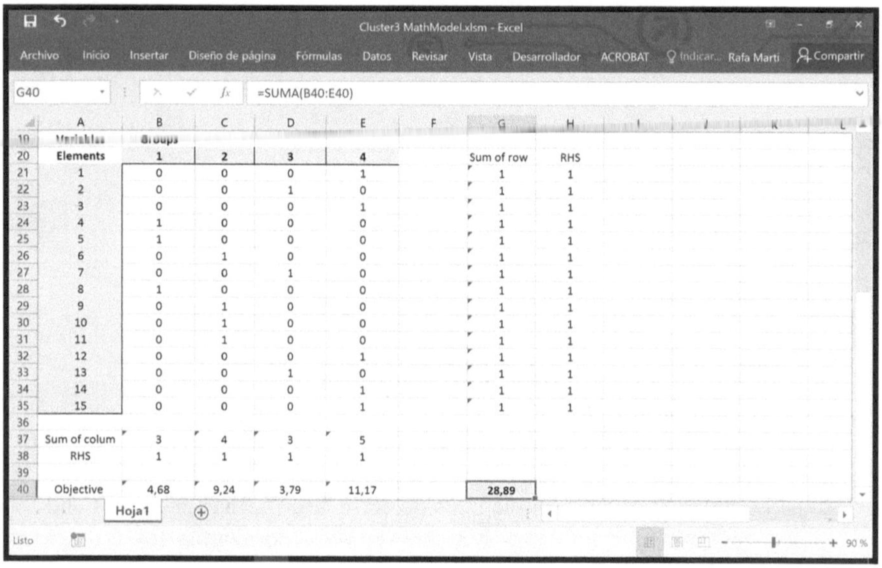

Fig. 4.3 Problem data

The Solver in Excel obtains the same solution than the one depicted in Fig. 4.2 obtained with the single linkage method. Note however that the mathematical model of this example with $n = 15$ and $C = 4$ is very small, since it only has 60 variables and 19 constraints. The Solver in Excel can only handle problems with up to 200 variables, and therefore even a clustering problem of small size, say for instance with $n = 40$ and $C = 6$, cannot be solved with this method. Additionally, it is well known that when the number of binary variables approaches 200, the running time becomes relatively long. We therefore propose a metaheuristic method to obtain good solutions for medium and large clustering problems in short computational times. It is based on the tabu search methodology, described in the next section.

4.4 The Tabu Search Methodology

Tabu search is a meta-heuristic that guides a local heuristic search procedure to explore the solution space beyond local optimality by allowing non-improving moves. Chapter 3 describes how a local search method operates by performing moves as long as the current solution improves. This standard local search method stops when no further improvement is possible. The tabu search methodology provides rules and mechanisms to keep performing moves from this point. Instead of stopping the search, the method specifies to perform moves even if they result in worse solutions than the current one. Additional mechanisms, based on memory structures, are implemented in a local search to avoid cycling. The name *tabu* comes from the fact that move selection is limited because certain moves or solutions are forbidden (declared tabu) as a result of the recent history (or trajectory) of the search.

Tabu search (TS) uses *attributive memory* for guiding purposes. This type of memory records information about solution attributes that change in moving from one solution to another. For example, in a graph or network setting, attributes can consist of nodes or arcs that are added or dropped by the moving mechanism. In production scheduling, the index of jobs may be used as attributes to inhibit or encourage the method to follow certain search directions. The attributive term means that we are not going to record all the solutions generated (because we are not interested in examining all the solutions of the problem) but we are going to record some of their properties (attributes). This attributive memory not only prevents the cycling in the search, but it turns out to perform a very efficient exploration of the solution space.

We now create an algorithm based on tabu search principles to obtain a good solution for our clustering problem. The first step is to obtain a solution from which to initiate the search process. Since the tabu search method is not very dependent on the initial solution, we can create a straightforward initial solution to save computational effort.

4.4.1 The Initial Solution

Consider that we want to create $k = 4$ clusters, called C_1, C_2, C_3, and C_4, in our example with $n = 15$ elements. A simple constructive method is to assign the elements to the clusters iteratively. For example we can assign consecutively four elements to the first three clusters, obtaining $C_1 = \{1, 2, 3, 4\}$, $C_2 = \{5, 6, 7, 8\}$, and $C_3 = \{9, 10, 11, 12\}$, and assign the remaining three elements to the fourth cluster: $C_4 = \{13, 14, 15\}$. This initial solution does not rely on the distances among elements, and therefore it is expected that it does not have a good value. However, it gives us the opportunity to illustrate the ability of the tabu search method to reach high quality solutions independently of the quality of the initial solution.

In this section we implement this simple constructive method in Visual Basic (VB). The file *Cluster3 VB.xlsm* contains the associated VB macro. As described in Chap. 3, to start the code we first have to create a command button to launch the Visual Basic editor. We refer the reader to the code in Chap. 3 to set up the *Developer Tab* on the Excel ribbon to type the code. Note that most of the Visual Basic instructions that we are going to use in this section were introduced and described in Chap. 3. We therefore recommend the reader to study first the code in Chap. 3 before reading this one.

To create the code of our method, we first define the vectors and variables to store the elements of the solution. Since we do not know beforehand how many elements will finally be in each cluster, we consider a maximum number of 10 in the cluster definition. To simplify this definition, we create the matrix `Cluster` with 4 rows and 10 columns, where each row stores the elements of each cluster. In this way, `Cluster(1,3)` records the third element in C_1. Since the number of elements in each cluster may change during the search, we also need a variable to record this number. Specifically, we define the vector `num` with four entries, each one corresponding to the number of elements in each cluster.

```
Dim Cluster(4, 10) As Integer
Dim num(4) As Integer
```

To implement the simple constructive method described above, we first compute the number m of elements in the first clusters ($m = n/k$). To round up the quotient and to obtain and integer value, we use the VB expression `m = Int(n / k) + 1`. Then, we assign the resulting m as the number of elements in each cluster with `num(i) = m`. The fourth cluster receives the remaining elements, which turns out to be `num(4) = n - 3 * m`, as shown in the first block of the code below. Then, we iteratively assign an element `cont` to each cluster. In the first `For` instruction of the second block in the code below, the cluster variable `c` goes from 1 to `k`, while in the second (inner) `For`, the variable `i` is the index of the elements in each cluster. Starting with `cont=1`, the procedure assigns each element to the cluster in the instruction `Cluster(c, i) = cont`, and then increment `cont` by one unit to be ready for the next assignment.

```
m = Int(n / k) + 1
For i = 1 To 3
    num(i) = m
Next i
num(4) = n - 3 * m

cont = 1
For c = 1 To k
For i = 1 To num(c)
          Cluster(c, i) = cont
          cont = cont + 1
Next i
Next c
```

Once a solution has been created, we have to evaluate it (i.e., we have to compute the objective function value of this solution). The following code shows how to evaluate our solution by adding to the variable `Value` the distance of every pair of points in each cluster. To this end, the `c` variable in the outer `For` loop explores the clusters from 1 to `k`. In each cluster, the variables `i` and `j` examine the elements to compute their associate distance.

```
Value = 0
For c = 1 To k
    For i = 1 To num(c) - 1
    For j = i + 1 To num(c)
        a = Cluster(c, i)
        b = Cluster(c, j)
        Value = Value + Cells(a, b)
    Next j
    Next i
Next c
```

4.4.2 Short Term Memory

Tabu search begins in the same way as an ordinary local or neighborhood search, proceeding iteratively from one solution to another until a chosen termination criterion is satisfied. When TS is applied to an optimization problem with the objective of minimizing or maximizing $f(x)$ subject to $x \in X$, each solution x has an associated neighborhood $\mathcal{N}(x)$, and each solution $y \in \mathcal{N}(x)$ can be reached from x by an operation called a *move*. This is the same principle described in the local search of Chap. 3.

When contrasting TS with a simple descent method where the goal is to minimize $f(x)$, we must point out that such a method only permits moves to neighbor solutions that improve the current objective function value and ends when no improving solutions can be found. Tabu search, on the other hand, permits moves that deteriorate the current objective function value but the moves are chosen from a modified neighborhood $\mathcal{N}^*(x)$. Short and long term memory structures are responsible for the specific composition of $\mathcal{N}^*(x)$. In other words, the modified neighborhood is the result of maintaining a selective history of the states encountered during the search.

In short term memory we usually consider attributes of the solutions recently visited, or the moves performed, in the last iterations. These attributes are used to exclude some elements in the neighborhood of the solutions in the next iterations. $\mathcal{N}^*(x)$ is typically a subset of $\mathcal{N}(x)$, and the *tabu classification* serves to identify elements of $\mathcal{N}(x)$ excluded from $\mathcal{N}^*(x)$. Let $\mathcal{T}(x)$ be this set of solutions in $\mathcal{N}(x)$, labeled as tabu, that we do not consider admissible for selection, i.e.,

$$\mathcal{N}^*(x) = \mathcal{N}(x) \setminus \mathcal{T}(x).$$

Recency based memory, as its name suggests, keeps track of attributes of solutions that have changed during the recent past. To exploit this memory, selected attributes that occur in solutions recently visited are labeled *tabu-active*, and solutions that contain tabu-active elements, or particular combinations of these attributes, are those that become tabu, thus being included in $\mathcal{T}(x)$. This prevents certain solutions from the recent past from belonging to $\mathcal{N}^*(x)$ and hence from being revisited. Algorithm 4 shows an outline of a tabu search method with a simple short term memory according to the description above. Note that the concept of *best* in line 6 of the algorithm considers the possibility of $f(y)$ being worse than $f(x)$. This is why in step 8 we check if y is better than the best solution found so far, x^*. This is important because in pure local search the current solution is also the best solution. However, in TS the best solution is not necessary the current solution. The method finishes in step 11 by returning the best solution found.

Algorithm 4: Short term tabu search

1: Generate an initial solution x
2: Set $x^* = x$
3: Determine the attributes to establish the tabu status of solutions
4: **while** The stopping condition is not satisfied **do**
5:     Compute $\mathcal{T}(x)$ and set $\mathcal{N}^*(x) = \mathcal{N}(x) \setminus \mathcal{T}(x)$
6:     Let y be the best solution in $\mathcal{N}^*(x)$
7:     Set $x = y$
8:     If y is better than x^*, then $x^* = y$
9:     Update the tabu status of solutions
10: **end while**
11: Return x^*

In the clustering problem a solution is formed by a set of clusters, each one containing some of the elements. In particular in our example with $n = 15$ elements and $k = 4$ clusters, we consider the initial solution given by $C_1 = \{1,2,3,4\}$, $C_2 = \{5,6,7,8\}$, $C_3 = \{9,10,11,12\}$, and $C_4 = \{13,14,15\}$.

We can define different types of moves for the clustering problem which would result in different tabu search algorithms. A basic move for this problem is the so-called *insertion* in which an element is removed from its cluster and inserted in another cluster. For example, in the initial solution we can remove element 2 from C_1 and insert it in C_2 resulting in the solution $C_1 = \{1,3,4\}$, $C_2 = \{2,5,6,7,8\}$, $C_3 = \{9,10,11,12\}$, and $C_4 = \{13,14,15\}$. We now would evaluate the new solution and compare this value with the value of the original solution. Note that we can evaluate a solution after a move in an incremental way (i.e., from the value of the original solution). To update the value when we remove an element from a cluster, we have to subtract the sum of the distances from this element to the rest of the elements in the cluster. Symmetrically, since this element goes to another cluster, we have to add to the value, the sum of the distances between this element and the rest of the elements in the new cluster. The difference between the added and subtracted values is called the *move value* and provides the increment or decrease of the objective function if the move is performed.

4.4.3 The Visual Basic Macro

The following code computes the sum of the distances from an element `a` in a cluster `c`, to the rest of the elements in this cluster. As mentioned above, this amount, stored in the variable `a_value_in_c` has to be subtracted from the solution value when the element is removed from this cluster.

```
a_value_in_c = 0
For j = 1 To num(c)
    b = Cluster(c, j)
    a_value_in_c = a_value_in_c + Cells(a, b)
Next j
```

In a similar way, the following code computes the value `a_value_in_c2` that has to be added to the value of the current solution, when element `a` is inserted in cluster `c2`.

```
a_value_in_c2 = 0
For j = 1 To num(c2)
    b = Cluster(c2, j)
    a_value_in_c2 = a_value_in_c2 + Cells(a, b)
Next j
```

With both variables we can compute the move value as:

```
move_value = a_value_in_c2 - a_value_in_c
```

If the move value is negative, it indicates that `a_value_in_c` is larger than `a_value_in_c2`, thus the move is able to reduce the total sum of distances within clusters. In other words, it is an improving move.

A standard way to explore the neighborhood of a solution is the *best* strategy, in which all the neighbor solutions are examined in search for the best one. In our problem, it means that, given a solution, we consider to move, one by one, every element from its current cluster, inserting it in a different cluster. The following code implements this strategy to identify the best move associated with the current solution. To do this, we create the `best_move` variable to check, for every candidate move, if its move value is larger than the best found so far, in order to identify the best one in the neighborhood.

The outer `For` loop of the code below scans the clusters, from `c=1` to `k`, from which to remove an element `a`. Similarly, the second `For` scans the clusters in search for the cluster `c2` to insert `a`. The third `For` explores the elements in cluster `c`, assigning them to the variable in the instruction `a= Cluster(c,i)`. Then, the move value is computed from the variables `a_value_in_c` and `a_value_in_c2` as indicated above.

```
For c = 1 To k
For c2 = 1 To k
    For i = 1 To num(c)

    a = Cluster(c, i)

    a_value_in_c = 0
    For j = 1 To num(c)
        b = Cluster(c,j)
        a_value_in_c = a_value_in_c + Cells(a,b)
    Next j

    a_value_in_c2 = 0
    For j = 1 To num(c2)
        b = Cluster(c2,j)
        a_value_in_c2 = a_value_in_c2 + Cells(a,b)
    Next j

    ' IDENTIFY BEST NON-TABU MOVE
    move_value = a_value_in_c2 - a_value_in_c
    If move_value < best_move And iter - tabu(a) > tenure Then
        best_move = move_value
        best_i = i
        best_a = a
        best_c = c
        best_c2 = c2
    End If

    Next i
Next c2
Next c
```

In a standard local search algorithm, when we identify the best move in a neighborhood and calculate its move value, if it is negative (i.e., if it is an improving move), we make it. In a tabu search algorithm however, we are not allowed to make tabu moves (i.e, moves that contain tabu attributes). To check the tabu status of the move in our code we include the `tabu` array. When an element `a` is moved from one cluster to another, we record in `tabu(a)` the number of the iteration in which the move took place. Then, we do not allow to move again this element during a certain number of iterations, called *tabu tenure*.

As mentioned above, the key feature of a tabu search method is to exclude from the neighborhood those solutions labeled as tabu. In other words, we do not permit to incorporate a tabu attribute in the solution. In our problem, we consider that the element moved (from one cluster to another) in recent iterations cannot be moved again. However, after a certain number of iterations (*tenure* iterations), we forget about the tabu status, and permit to move the element again. This is why it is called *Short Term Memory*. Note that the there are many choices to declare an attribute as tabu. We have considered here the moved element, but this is a design option and a different option could be considered. For instances, we can forbid an element `a` from returning to cluster `c`, instead of forbidding `a` from moving at all.

The instruction `iter-tabu(a)>tenure` checks the tabu status in our code above. It compares the current iteration number (`iter`) with the number of the iteration in which element `a` was declared tabu. If this difference is larger than `tenure`, it indicates that the tabu status has expired and we can perform the associated move. However, instead of immediately making the move, we record the information about this move in order to identify the best non-tabu move in the neighborhood. In particular, we record the move value, the element, and its index in the variables `best_move`, `best_a`, and `best_i` respectively. Similarly, the number of the clusters in the move are stored in `best_c` and `best_c2`. These variables are updated each time that a better non-tabu move is found. When all the moves have been examined, we use these variables to perform the best non-tabu move. Note that we do not check whether this move improves or not the solution. The tabu search method always performs the best non-tabu move, even if it deteriorates the current solution. The following code is executed just after the previous one to perform the move. Specifically, we increase by one unit the number of elements in the cluster `best_c2`, add element `best_a`, decrease by one unit the number of elements in cluster `best_c`, and remove element `best_a` from `best_c`. We shift the rest of the elements in cluster `best_c` not to leave blank spaces in the cluster array `Cluster`. Finally, we update the value of the solution by making `Value=Value+best_move`, and record in `tabu(best_a)` the number of the current iteration `iter` to forbid moving again `best_a` in the next iterations.

```
num(best_c2) = num(best_c2) + 1
Cluster(best_c2, num(best_c2)) = best_a
For j = best_i To num(best_c)
    Cluster(best_c, j) = Cluster(best_c, j + 1)
Next j
num(best_c) = num(best_c) - 1
Value = Value + best_move
tabu(best_a) = iter
```

Since the move performed with the code above can produce a solution worse than the current one, we have to keep track of the best solution found by the algorithm. In this way, when the search time expires, or in general when the stopping criterion is met, the algorithm returns the best solution found as the output. If we execute the

Visual Basic macro containing this code in the *Cluster3 VB.xlsm* file, we obtain the same solution obtained in the previous chapters: $C_1 = \{4,5,8\}, C_2 = \{6,9,10,11\}$, $C_3 = \{2,7,13\}$, and $C_4 = \{1,3,12,14,15\}$. It has an objective function value (sum of intra cluster distances) of 28.88. Note that this code can be applied to other instances obtaining high-quality solutions in seconds.

We did not include in this description, and in the associated Visual Basic implementation, the so-called *aspiration criteria*. In general terms, this is a rule or a set of rules that permit to override the tabu status under certain conditions. In simple tabu search implementations an aspiration criterion allows the method to make a move if it results in a solution with an objective value better than that of the current best-known solution even if it is tabu. We have empirically found that in our Visual Basic code we do not need this rule to reach high quality solutions.

4.4.4 Long Term Memory

If we conceptualize the search space as a huge set of solutions and realize that we are only able to explore a tiny part of it, we can easily understand the rationale behind the two search strategies *intensification* and *diversification* that are implemented over the long term. Roughly speaking, the first one favors the exploration of promising areas of the solution space, while the second one drives the search to new regions. Therefore, intensification and diversification have complementary objectives. Intensification strategies are based on modifying choice rules to encourage move combinations and solution features that have historically been found to be good. In some settings, they consist of revisiting attractive regions to search them more thoroughly. Diversification strategies, on the other hand, are based on visiting unexplored regions, increasing the effectiveness in exploring the solution space of search methods based on local optimization.

Most tabu search implementations limit themselves to Short Term Memory since it provides effective solving methods. In some cases, however, the method can benefit from the addition of long term memory and its associated strategies (intensification and diversification). We do not include here the Visual Basic code of these strategies but we describe them and include examples of their use.

Frequency-based memory provides a type of information that complements the information provided by recency-based memory. In the previous section we described how to record recent information and how to use it to guide the search. In particular, for our clustering problem, we proposed to record the element moved from one cluster to another and do not permit to move it again for a certain number of iterations. This is a short term or recent-based strategy that could be complemented with a longer term strategy. For example, we could record the number of times that an element has been moved and, after a relatively large number of iterations, consider to move those elements with a low number of previous moves. That would be a diversification strategy since its objective is to reach new solution regions of the solution space.

Frequencies typically consist of ratios, whose numerators represent counts expressed in two different measures: a *transition measure*, such as the number of iterations where an attribute changes (enters or leaves) the solutions visited, and a *residence measure*, such as the number of iterations where an attribute belongs to solutions visited on a particular trajectory. The denominators generally represent one of the following three types of quantities:

- The total number of associated iterations
- The sum (or average) of the numerators
- The maximum numerator value

The ratios produce transition frequencies that keep track of how often attributes change, and residence frequencies that keep track of how often attributes are members of solutions generated.

A key element of the adaptive memory framework of tabu search is to create a balance between search intensification and diversification. It is important to keep in mind that intensification and diversification are not mutually opposing, but are rather mutually reinforcing.

In our clustering problem a straightforward transition measure is the number of times that an element has been moved from a cluster to another. This frequency can be divided by the total number of moves performed, to obtain a ratio as a basis for a long term strategy. Similarly, a residence measure can be the number of solutions in which two elements belong to the same cluster. We can create a frequency matrix to record this information for all pairs of elements. Dividing these frequencies by the total number of solutions visited, provides a ratio that can also be seen as a percentage. With both frequency ratios we can modify the selection rules when exploring the neighborhood of a solution, to favor the exploration of non-visited solutions. For example we can penalize those solutions containing the elements already present in many solutions, to encourage the search to move to other types of solutions, different from those already visited. The term penalize refers to modifying the objective function by adding, in a minimization problem, a term to increase its value, making the solution less attractive.

4.5 Exercises

1. The Visual Basic code described in this chapter and collected in the Appendix implements a Short Term Memory based on a tabu list. The main loop in the code performs a large number of iterations (close to 5000). Perform several runs changing this number to find out the minimum number of iterations required to reach the best solution obtained with this method.

2. The tabu search method created in this chapter starts from a simple solution constructed in a straightforward way. We did it in that way since tabu search is not

dependent from the initial solution where the search is initiated. To test this point, we ask you to create a different initial solution and apply the same tabu search from it, in order to check if you reach the same best solution in that way. In particular, implement the following simple procedure which consists of selecting four observations to be the centroids of the four clusters. Then you assign the rest of the observations to the nearest centroid. The four seeds could be chosen by first selecting one and then the second one is the observations farthest away from the first. The third one is the observation farthest away from both the first one and the second one.

3. Complement the Short Term Memory Tabu Search with a Long Term Memory component. A possible implementation would consist of creating a frequency matrix `freq` to collect the number of times that two elements `i` and `j` have been in the same cluster (`freq(i,j)`). Then, at some point in the search (when the best solution found is not improved), penalize for a certain number of iterations the move evaluation to reach new solutions. In particular, when moving an element `i` from one cluster to another one, we can add to the move value a value proportional to the number of elements in the new cluster that have been in the same cluster than `i` for a large number of iterations (say larger than a threshold value). In this way, we favor the inclusion of `i` in a cluster with many elements that have not been with it (i.e., we favor the exploration of a new solution different in structure to those visited during the search).

Appendix: Visual Basic code

As we did in the previous chapter, we put together in this section all the code described in the previous sections. In this way, the reader can have a complete picture of how it works.

```
Private Sub CommandButton1_Click()

'CREATE DATA STRUCTURES

' CURRENT SOLUTION
Dim Cluster(4, 10) As Integer
Dim num(4) As Integer
Dim Value As Double

' BEST SOLUTION FOUND
Dim BValue As Range
Set BValue = Range("Q2")
Range("Q1").Value = "Value"
```

```
Dim BCluster As Range
Set BCluster = Range("U2:AD5")
Dim Bnum As Range
Set Bnum = Range("S2:S5")

'PROBLEM DIMENSION AND PARAMETERS
n = 15
k = 4

'TABU MEMORY
Dim tabu(15) As Integer
Dim tenure As Integer
tenure = 5

' COMPUTE THE INITIAL AND BEST SOLUTIONS
m = Int(n / k) + 1
For i = 1 To 3
    num(i) = m
    Bnum(i) = m
Next i
num(4) = n - 3 * m
Bnum(4) = n - 3 * m

cont = 1
For c = 1 To k
For i = 1 To num(c)
        Cluster(c, i) = cont
        BCluster(c, i) = cont
        cont = cont + 1
Next i
Next c

' COMPUTE THE INITIAL AND BEST VALUE
Value = 0
For c = 1 To k
    For i = 1 To num(c) - 1
    For j = i + 1 To num(c)
        a = Cluster(c, i)
        b = Cluster(c, j)
        Value = Value + Cells(a, b)
    Next j
    Next i
Next c
BValue = Value

' MAIN LOOP OF THE SEARCH
For iter = tenure + 1 To 5000

    best_move = 1000
    For c = 1 To k
    For c2 = 1 To k
        For i = 1 To num(c)
            a = Cluster(c, i)
```

```
            'VALUE TO REMOVE a FROM ITS CURRENT CLUSTER c
            a_value_in_c = 0
            For j = 1 To num(c)
                b = Cluster(c, j)
                a_value_in_c = a_value_in_c + Cells(a, b)
            Next j

            'VALUE TO ADD a TO ITS NEW CLUSTER c2
            a_value_in_c2 = 0
            For j = 1 To num(c2)
                b = Cluster(c2, j)
                a_value_in_c2 = a_value_in_c2 + Cells(a, b)
            Next j

            ' IDENTIFY BEST NON-TABU MOVE
            move_value = a_value_in_c2 - a_value_in_c
            If move_value < best_move And iter - tabu(a) > tenure Then
                best_move = move_value
                best_i = i
                best_a = a
                best_c = c
                best_c2 = c2
            End If
       Next i
    Next c2
    Next c

    ' PERFORM THE BEST NON-TABU MOVE
    num(best_c2) = num(best_c2) + 1
    Cluster(best_c2, num(best_c2)) = best_a
    For j = best_i To num(best_c)
         Cluster(best_c, j) = Cluster(best_c, j + 1)
    Next j
    num(best_c) = num(best_c) - 1
    Value = Value + best_move
    tabu(best_a) = iter

    'UPDATE BEST SOLUTION
    If BValue > Value Then
        BValue = Value
        For c = 1 To k
            Bnum(c) = num(c)
            For i = 1 To 10
                BCluster(c, i) = Cluster(c, i)
            Next i
        Next c
    End If
Next iter
End Sub
```

References

1. Duarte, A., M. Laguna, and R. Martí. 2011. Tabu search for the linear ordering problem with cumulative costs. *Computational Optimization and Applications* 48: 697–715.
2. Gendreau, M., and Potvin, J. Y. (eds.) 2010. *Handbook of metaheuristics*. International Series in Operations Research and Management Science (vol. 146). Berlin: Springer.
3. Glover, F. 1977. Heuristics for integer programming using surrogate constraints. *Decision Sciences* 8: 371–392.
4. Glover, F., and Laguna, M. 1997. *Tabu search*. Dordrecht: Kluwer Academic Publishers.
5. Hertz, A., and M. Widmer. 2003. Guidelines for the use of meta-heuristics in combinatorial optimization. *European Journal of Operational Research* 151: 247–252.
6. Martí, R., M. Laguna, F. Glover, and V. Campos. 2001. Reducing the bandwidth of a sparse matrix with tabu search. *European Journal of Operational Research* 135: 450–459.

Chapter 5
Black-Box Solvers

Linear programming is perhaps the best-known tool for optimization. Linear programming is a general-purpose framework that allows a real system to be abstracted as a model with a linear objective function subject to a set of linear constraints. The state-of-the-art linear programming solvers are quite powerful and are capable of solving models with thousands of decision variables employing a reasonable amount of computer effort. However, not all business and industrial problems can be expressed by means of a linear objective and linear constraints in the form of equalities or inequalities. Many complex systems may not even have a convenient mathematical representation, linear or nonlinear. Techniques such as linear programming and its relatives (nonlinear programming and integer programming) generally require a number of simplifying assumptions about the real system to be able to fit the problem within the framework.

Linear programming solvers are designed to exploit the structure of a well-defined and carefully studied problem. The disadvantage to the user is that in order to formulate the problem as a linear program, simplifying assumptions and abstractions may be necessary. This leads to the well-known dilemma of either finding the optimal solution to models that are not accurate representations of the real system or developing models that are good abstractions of the real system but for which only inferior solutions can be obtained with existing methods. When dealing with difficult optimization problems, a course of action taken for many years has been to develop simple heuristics and rules-of-thumb that, in general, did not require a mathematical formulation of the problem. These procedures are appealing from the standpoint of simplicity, but they generally lack the power to provide high quality solutions to complex problems.

Metaheuristics provide a way of considerably improving the performance of simple heuristic procedures. The search strategies proposed by metaheuristic methodologies result in iterative procedures with the ability to explore solution spaces beyond the solutions that result from applying a simple heuristic. As we have discussed, some metaheuristics are designed to operate on a set of solutions that is

A. Duarte et al., *Metaheuristics for Business Analytics*, EURO Advanced Tutorials on Operational Research, https://doi.org/10.1007/978-3-319-68119-1_5

maintained from iteration to iteration, while others maintain only one solution by applying mechanisms to transform the current solution into a new one. Metaheuristics of both types have been developed to solve complex optimization problems in many areas, with combinatorial optimization being one of the most fruitful. By and large, the most efficient procedures achieve their efficiencies by relying on context information, that is, by taking advantage of specific information about the problem. The solution approach is the result of adapting metaheuristic strategies to specific optimization problems. In this case, there is no separation between the solution procedure and the model that represents the optimization problem.

Chapters 3 and 4 described the process followed to create specialized procedures to search for high-quality solutions to optimization problems employing several heuristic methodological frameworks. Specialized procedures tend to perform very well for the problem that they are tackling because they take advantage of context information. That is, the design elements are linked to the problem being solved. The solution representation, the moves, the search strategies, and the evaluation are designed specifically to be effective for the particular problem context. The specialization and the resulting efficiencies are the advantages of creating problem-specific solutions using metaheuristic technology. The main disadvantage, however, is that a new procedure must be created every time a new problem arises. Development time could be saved by adapting elements from previous implementations. Still, the end result is that there is a fair amount of coding and testing that has to happen to create solutions to new problems.

Metaheuristics can also be used to create solution procedures that are context independent, that is, procedures capable of tackling several problem classes and that use either limited or no specific information from the problem in order to customize the search. The original genetic algorithmic designs, for example, were based on this paradigm, where solutions to all problems were represented as a string of zeros and ones. The advantage of this particular design is that the same solver can be used to tackle a wide variety of problems, because the solver uses strategies to manipulate the string of zeros and ones and a decoder is used to translate the string into a solution to the problem under consideration. The obvious disadvantage is that the solutions found by context-independent solvers tend to be inferior to those of specialized procedures when applying the same amount of computer effort (e.g., search time).

We make the distinction between general-purpose and black-box solvers as follows. We refer to general-purpose solvers as those that can be applied to a general class of problems. For instance, CPLEX is a general-purpose solver for linear (LP), integer (IP), and mixed-integer (MIP) programming problems. These solvers know some characteristics of the problems that are designed to solve. For example, LP solvers expect models with a linear objective function, a linear set of up to three types of constraints (less-than-or-equal, equal, and more-than-or-equal), and a set of continuous variables. Black-box solvers, on the other hand, do not have any information about the problem being solved other than the type of decision variables. Black-box solvers rely on an evaluation model (i.e., the black box) that takes care of modeling the problem. Black box optimizers are also referred to as context-independent solvers.

Context-independence is difficult to define because no solver is totally independent from the context. Solvers are developed within a spectrum that ranges from almost no dependence on context to total dependence on context. Knowledge about the context may relate to the objective function or to the set constraints. For instance, some solvers may not have information about the structure of the objective function but have information about the feasibility region as defined by a set of constraints. Mathematical programming approaches, for instance, exploit very specific structures, even though they dont know? the exact nature of the problem that they are solving (i.e., the problem could be related to workforce planning, or investment allocation, etc.). The structure and therefore context dependency is given by the formulation and not by the unknown (to the solver) real world context.

Nonlinear optimization approaches that do not use derivatives (or estimate them) to find search directions such as Nelder and Mead or Powell may be considered as being at the high level of the context-independence range because they treat the objective function as a black box. Methods that estimate derivatives like those based on generalized reduced gradients (GRG) assume objective function smoothness and that assumption alone moves them closer to the context-dependence end of the spectrum. In practice, however, some of these procedures (for example the standard version of Microsoft Excels Solver) are routinely used to search for solutions to problems that do not meet the smoothness requirement.

General-purpose and black-box solvers are the alternative to creating specialized procedures. The black box nomenclature refers to the problem model, where the input is the set of decision variables and the output is the objective function value.[1] Figure 5.1 shows a graphical representation of the black-box model for optimization.

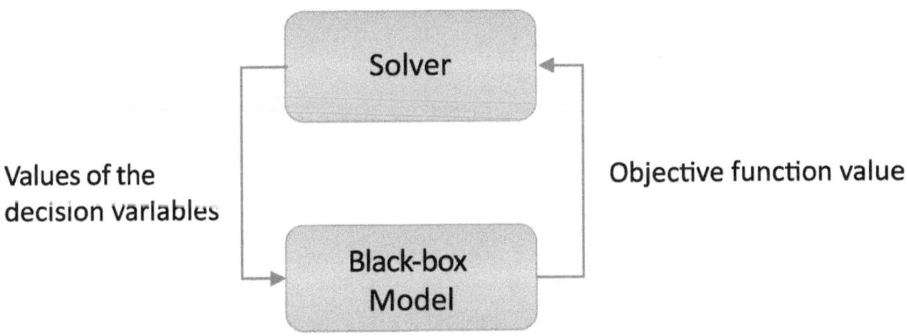

Fig. 5.1 Black-box optimization

[1] In general, black boxes can produce more than one output that can be used, for example, in multiobjective optimization model. Outputs from black boxes could also be used to set up constraints. This is typical in settings such as those in which a black box is a computer simulation. For the purpose of this book, however, we will limit our discussion to black boxes that produce a single output that is used as the objective function value.

As shown in Fig. 5.1, in black-box optimization, there is a complete separation between the solution procedure (Solver) and the model that represents the problem (Black box). One of the main design considerations when developing a general-purpose optimizer is the solution representation to be employed. The solution representation is used to establish the communication between the solver and the solution evaluator (i.e., the black box). As mentioned above, classical genetic algorithms used binary strings to represent solutions. This representation may not be particularly convenient in all instances but it has the advantage that almost anything can be expressed as a string of zeros and ones and then mapped to a solution of a problem. There is a tradeoff between solution representations that are generic and those that are specific. General-purpose optimizers often incorporate more than one representation and at least one of these allows for maximum flexibility. In addition to binary variables, another popular representation is a n-dimensional vector x, where each component x_i (for $i = 1, \ldots, n$) is a continuous or integer bounded variable. This representation can be used in a wide range of applications, which include all those problems that can be formulated as mathematical programs. Other applications might not be immediately obvious. For example, consider a situation where one wishes to solve a sequencing problem employing a general-purpose optimizer that represents solutions as x. Let us assume that a sequence-evaluation code (or a spreadsheet) exists that uses a solution representation for which s_i is the index of the ith element in the sequence. The sequence evaluator takes s as an input and produces the objective function value as an output. In this hypothetical situation, let us also assume that the x variables are continuous and bounded between 0 and 1. The solver then generates values for x, where the value of x_i may be interpreted as the "priority" of element i. Therefore, as far as the general-purpose solver is concerned, the problem to be solved consists of assigning a value between 0 and 1 to n variables. Since $x = \{x_1, \ldots, x_n\}$ does not represent a solution to a sequencing problem, the decoding $x \rightarrow s$ must be performed before the objective function value can be calculated by the black box. This type of mapping is done in the methodology known as random-key genetic algorithms.

One naïve decoder could order the x variables according to their value and use this order as the sequence. The main disadvantage of this process is that it does not result in a one-to-one mapping of x into s. There are many solutions in the x space that map to the same solution in the s space. For instance, the solutions $\{0.378, 0.456, 0.123, 0.965\}$ and $\{0.786, 0.836, 0.623, 0.885\}$ represent the same sequence $\{3, 1, 2, 4\}$. The many-to-one mapping creates inefficiencies when searching for solutions to this problem with a general-purpose optimizer based on continuous variables between 0 and 1, given that there is nothing to prevent the search from constructing solutions x that map to sequences s that have already been considered. This simple example shows the importance of selecting an appropriate solution representation and decoder when modeling and solving problems with black-box optimization.

5.1 Excel's Evolutionary Solver

The exercises in Chap. 2 are examples of black-box optimization. In each of the exercises, the spreadsheet model is the black box on which the Evolutionary solver operates. The spreadsheet model is a black box because the Evolutionary Solver has no particular knowledge of the problem and it has not been specialized to solve it. The information that is given to the Evolutionary Solver is summarized by the solution representation (i.e., the type of decisions variables or changing cells) and the set of constraints. The decision variables can be binary, discrete, or continuous. As discussed in Sect. 2.3, constraints determine the feasible region of the solution space. In the black-box model, constraints may be enforced by the solver to ensure that all combinations of decision variable values are feasible before being evaluated by the black box. Alternatively, the black box could be designed to handle infeasible solutions using penalty functions (as described in Sect. 2.3). Before discussing these two alternatives for handling constraints, let us illustrate with the following example how models that are not black box handle constrained optimization problems.

Example 5.1 A common problem in supply chain management consists of assigning customers to facilities in order to either maximize revenue or minimize cost. Facilities have limited capacity and each customer has a capacity requirement that depends on the facility to which it is assigned. The problem has two sets of constraints: (1) each customer must be assigned to one facility only and (2) the sum of the requirements of all the customers assigned to a facility should not exceed the capacity of the facility. Table 5.1 shows the revenue and resources associated with a problem with 20 customers and 5 facilities.

Assume that the resource capacity is 42, 54, 52, 47, and 55 for each facility, respectively. This problem can be formulated as a 0-1 integer programming problem by defining x_{ij} variables representing the assignment of a customer j to a facility i. That is, x_{ij} equals one if customer j is assigned to facility i and it equals zero otherwise. Table 5.2 shows the customer assignment that maximizes revenue.

The total revenue associated with the solution shown in Table 5.2 is 434. Facility 1 serves 5 customers, facilities 2–4 serve 4 customers, and facility 5 serves 3 customers. It can be easily verified, by inspecting the numbers in the last column in Table 5.2, that the solution is feasible with respect to the resource capacity in each facility. The total requirements at each facility do not exceed the requirement capacities. It can also be verified that all the customers have been assigned to one facility. Since the objective function is linear and all the constraints are also linear equations, the problem was solved with the well-known branch and bound solution technique. The solution shown in Table 5.2 was found with the Simplex LP solver in Excel, which guarantees the optimality of the solution found. The spreadsheet model, in this case, does not represent a black box because the solver is specialized for the type of problem that we have formulated. The constraints are explicitly handled by

Table 5.1 Revenue and resource requirement data for Example 5.1

	Customers																			
Facilities	1	2	3	4	5	6	7	8	9	10	11	12	13	14	15	16	17	18	19	20
Revenue																				
1	15	12	16	15	20	18	11	14	23	14	18	13	11	15	17	18	20	11	20	24
2	22	14	10	15	12	21	24	16	17	22	11	15	18	15	18	23	22	23	21	13
3	25	11	22	10	22	17	22	12	21	21	16	14	23	21	14	17	25	18	15	15
4	23	13	14	25	21	18	23	19	17	18	20	20	22	24	23	13	17	22	20	21
5	15	25	22	14	17	21	16	21	20	12	15	18	17	21	20	20	13	14	23	14
Resource requirements																				
1	11	11	5	25	10	17	16	20	5	20	14	10	15	6	11	14	13	8	15	11
2	17	17	12	23	16	25	13	16	19	16	24	17	21	6	6	10	23	21	5	18
3	13	13	20	17	8	7	16	9	23	18	21	24	11	15	12	24	19	23	13	12
4	6	10	18	16	12	25	17	7	10	6	20	20	9	20	11	21	6	9	20	23
5	7	14	18	24	7	24	18	19	18	23	15	16	14	9	16	25	15	20	23	17

Table 5.2 Customer assignment that maximizes total revenue

	Customers																				Required resources
Facilities	1	2	3	4	5	6	7	8	9	10	11	12	13	14	15	16	17	18	19	20	
1	0	0	1	0	0	0	0	0	1	0	1	0	0	1	0	0	0	0	0	1	41
2	0	0	0	0	0	0	1	0	0	1	0	0	0	0	0	1	0	0	1	0	50
3	1	0	0	0	1	0	0	0	0	0	0	0	1	0	0	0	1	0	0	0	51
4	0	0	0	1	0	0	0	1	0	0	0	0	0	0	1	0	0	1	0	0	43
5	0	1	0	0	0	1	0	0	0	0	0	1	0	0	0	0	0	0	0	0	54

the branch and bound method and the search, which is a form of partial enumeration, is conducted entirely in the feasible region of the solution space. The spreadsheet model and the associated Solver model can be found in *Example5.1.xlsx*.

Example 5.2 A more complex version of the assignment problem described in Example 5.1 includes a cost component at each facility. The cost is related to managing the inventory generated by the fulfillment of the orders placed by the customers assigned to the facility. This cost is nonlinear with respect to the demand. Specifically, the cost at facility i, denoted by f_i, has the following mathematical form:

$$f_i = h_i \sqrt{\sum_{j=1}^{n} d_{ij} x_{ij}}$$

The facility cost equation multiplies the square root of the sum of the total demand at the facility by the handling cost coefficient h_i. The demand of a customer i at facility j is denoted by d_{ij}. The optimization problem is to find an assignment that maximizes profit, which is calculated as the difference between total revenue and the cost at the facilities. Table 5.3 shows the demand values for each facility-customer combination.

Table 5.3 Demand for each customer at each facility

	Customers																			
Facilities	1	2	3	4	5	6	7	8	9	10	11	12	13	14	15	16	17	18	19	20
Demand																				
1	18	9	14	10	18	18	12	22	19	15	21	20	7	14	15	6	13	15	18	15
2	10	23	23	23	24	6	14	7	16	13	23	6	7	7	21	11	24	17	16	23
3	15	6	13	13	18	7	22	19	18	6	23	9	10	13	21	23	24	17	16	15
4	25	7	13	9	23	14	20	9	16	18	22	8	12	13	9	7	11	7	9	19
5	15	12	10	8	22	17	13	21	11	10	6	20	17	11	10	24	21	18	12	7

Assume that the handling costs at the five facilities are 4, 6, 7, 5, and 8, respectively. Then, the cost associated with the solution in Table 5.2 can be calculated as shown in Table 5.4.

Table 5.4 Facility cost calculation for Example 5.2

Facility	Total demand	Square root of the demand	Handling cost	Facility cost
1	83	9.11	4	36.44
2	54	7.35	6	44.09
3	67	8.19	7	57.3
4	34	5.83	5	29.15
5	49	7.00	8	56
			Total	222.98

The profit that corresponds to the solution in Table 5.2 is $434 - 222.98 = 211.02$. The addition of the facility cost in Example 5.2 results in a nonlinear binary optimization problem. The problem can no longer be solved with the Simplex LP solver, which requires the formulation to be linear in both the objective function and the constraint set. Several options are available at this point in order to find a high quality (perhaps optimal) solution to this problem:

1. Apply the Evolutionary Solver to the binary model which includes an explicit formulation of the two sets of constraints.

2. Change the solution representation to twenty x variables, where x_j represents the index of the facility to which customer j is assigned. Include the capacity restriction in the formulation for the solver to handle it.
3. Change the solution representation as in #2 but transform the capacity constraint into a function that penalizes solutions that violate the capacity restrictions.

The workbook *Example5.2.xlsx* contains the models for these three options. In the first model (Example 6.2.1 tab), the Evolutionary Solver is not capable of finding a solution that could satisfy both sets of constraints. This occurs when no initial solution is given. That is, all the assignment cells are blank when the solver is launched. In the second model (Example 6.2.2 tab), the black box (i.e., the spreadsheet model) is set up to take as an input 20 integer values in the range from 1 to 5, indicating the facility to which each customer is assigned. This input is transformed into the binary representation of the solution (see Table 5.2) in order to evaluate the resource requirements and the objective function. Because the solution representation that the solver uses implicitly satisfies the assignment constraints, the only constraint that is declared in the optimization model is the one associated with the resource requirements. The changing cells are declared integer and the limits are set to 1 and 5. Once again the solver fails to find a feasible solution.

Finally, an unconstrained optimization model is formulated (Example 6.2.3 tab). This model uses the previously described discrete-value solution representation but this time a penalty function is added to deal with the resource constraints. The objective function is calculated as the total profit minus a penalty term. The penalty term is the sum of the constraint violations multiplied by a penalty factor of 30. This factor is large enough to eliminate infeasible solutions with attractive profit values and small violations of the capacity constraints. The Evolutionary Solver is now capable of finding feasible solutions. The best one that it finds has a total revenue of 410 and a cost of 189.78 for a profit of 220.22. Note that in terms of the profit value, this solution is better than the one found when the costs are ignored and the objective function focuses on maximizing revenue. As shown above, that solution has a revenue of 434 but the cost of 222.98 decreases the profit to 211.02.

These examples show the difficulties related to solving constrained problems with a black-box model. The unconstrained models typically have a very large search (and solution) space which could be perceived as a disadvantage in terms of finding a global optimal solution. However, the advantage of these models is that all the solutions that the solver generates are feasible and ready to be evaluated by the black box model.

5.2 LocalSolver

The Evolutionary Solver that is distributed with Excel has limited solving capabilities. Example 5.2 illustrates that the solvers performance suffers when the optimization problem is formulated to satisfy constraints. In general, the solver prefers that the black-box model deals with all the constraints and that the optimization model becomes unconstrained. This is typical of a black-box solver and this is why, some software developers, such as Innovation 24 (the creators of LocalSolver), have opted for creating more than one form of their optimizers. LocalSolver is a commercial optimization system that provides extremely robust performance across multiple classes of optimization problems.[2] LocalSolver is distributed both as general-purpose solver and as a black-box solver. The general-purpose solver provides a rich set of expressions for modeling purpose. The black-box solver provides three types of solution representations and expects that the problem will be modeled within the black box. LocalSolver searches solution spaces with strategies designed for single-solution heuristics. The general-purpose form of LocalSolver provides a modeling language that allows the analyst to create models for solving a wide variety of problems. For combinatorial optimization, solutions may be represented with binary variables, integer variables, or lists.

The search starts from a solution generated by a basic greedy randomized procedure. The search is then performed in the feasible region and moves are performed to transform one solution to another. For example, for binary problems, the moves consist of flipping the values of k variables (k-flip). As its name indicates, LocalSolver attempts to find local optima by way of standard descent (for minimization problems) techniques. The embedded heuristics allow the process to select non-improving moves in order to escape local optimality. These heuristics include probabilistic models such as those typical to the simulated annealing methodology. A large catalog of moves are available during the search and the selection of the moves to try is dynamically adjusted. Move types that have resulted in improved solutions during the search have a higher probability of being selected again. For instance, when a constraint is such that a sum of the binary variables must equal a constant, the system is able to identify that a feasibility preserving move consists of flipping an even number of variable values, half in one direction (e.g., from zero to one) and half in the other (from one to zero), and thus maintaining the value of the sum. Extensions of k-flip moves are included, based on strategies such as ejection chains and alternating paths. For the purpose of efficiency, for each constraint, a list of "increasing variables" and "decreasing variables" are maintained. An increasing variable is one that causes an increase in the sum if the variable value is flipped. The opposite is true for decreasing variables. Likewise, a data structure is created to keep a record of the list of constraints where each variable appears. These data structures are helpful to implement complex moves that preserve feasibility, for example a k-path move.

Figure 5.2 shows a 6-path move for which each variable belongs to exactly two constraints and there are 6 constraints in the path. For instance, x_1 belongs to constraints C_1 and C_6. The arrows next to each variable indicate the direction in which

[2]The original versions of LocalSolver were designed to tackle combinatorial optimization problems represented with binary variables. The latest version of LocalSolver (Version 6.5, released on July 29, 2016) includes capabilities for dealing with additional variable types. LocalSolver is free for academic uses and can be downloaded from http://www.localsolver.com/.

the variable is changing, where up indicates a move from zero to one, and down indicates a move from one to zero. A bar on top of a variable name indicates that the variable is currently set to zero. The effectiveness of LocalSolver is largely due to moves such as the one illustrated in Fig. 5.2 and extensions that go even further in terms of its level of complexity.

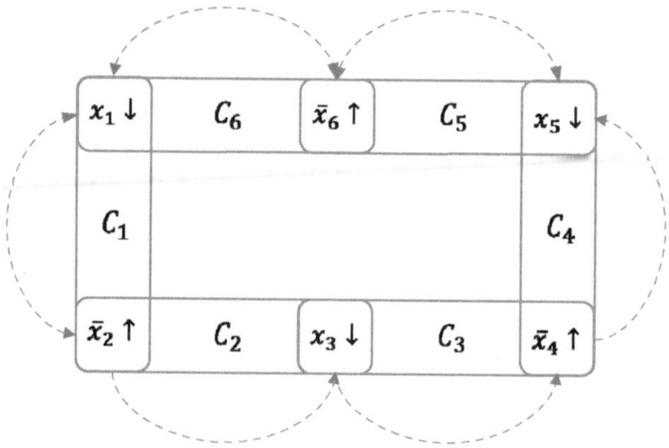

Fig. 5.2 Graphical representation of a 6-path move

An optimization model is represented within LocalSolver as directed acyclic graph (DAG), where the decision variables are the root nodes and the constraints and the objective functions are leave nodes. Each node in the DAG contains a type (e.g., sum, constant, variable, etc.) and a name. The operators used to model the problem induce the inner nodes. A solution is a complete instantiation of the root nodes. Evaluating a move using a DAG consists of changing the values of the root nodes and then propagating the modifications along the DAG.

Incremental evaluation is another key aspect of LocalSolvers search efficiency. Each node of the DAG is capable of initializing its value, evaluating a change, committing to a change, or rolling back to its original state. The initial value of a node depends on the value of its parents, before the local search starts. Once the local search starts, moves (i.e., changes on the variable values) need to be evaluated. The incremental evaluation is limited to those nodes that are impacted by the proposed change. The incremental evaluation of a node takes as an input the parent nodes that have changed and through clever mechanisms and efficient coding, the goal is that the evaluation is completed in a time that is a linear function of the number of impacted parents. If the move is accepted, then the value of the node is permanently changed. Otherwise, the value is rolled back.

The purpose of providing a high-level description of the LocalSolver strategies and implementation structures is to give the reader an idea of the complexity of creating a general-purpose solver. In addition to an efficient search engine, general-purpose solvers must provide a friendly interface. The modeling language within

LocalSolver is Local Search Programming (LSP). The language is richer than mathematical programming because it includes both logical and mathematical operators. The following example will help us illustrate some basic feature of LSP.

Example 5.3 Suppose that three jobs must be assigned to one of two machines (A and B). Once they are assigned to a machine, they can be processed in any order. The processing times of these jobs are 2, 3, and 4 hours respectively. A job with processing time of 5 hours is already assigned to machine B. The goal is to find the assignments of the three jobs in order to minimize the completion time of the machine that finishes last. Let us define x_{ij} as a binary variable that takes on the value of one when job i is assigned to machine j and zero otherwise. Then, the problem can be formulated as follows:

$$
\begin{aligned}
\min\ & c \\
\text{subject to}\ & x_{1A} + x_{1B} = 1 \\
& x_{2A} + x_{2B} = 1 \\
& x_{3A} + x_{3B} = 1 \\
& 2x_{1A} + 3x_{2A} + 4x_{3A} \leq c \\
& 2x_{1B} + 3x_{2B} + 4x_{3B} + 5 \leq c \\
& x_{ij} = \{0, 1\}
\end{aligned}
$$

Clearly, this "toy" problem could be either solved by trying all assignments or by formulating a 0-1 integer program for the Simplex LP solver in Excel. Alternatively, the problem may be formulated as a LocalSolver model as follows:

```
function model() {
  x1A <- bool(); x2A <- bool(); x3A <- bool();
  x1B <- bool(); x2B <- bool(); x3B <- bool();
  constraint x1A + x1B == 1;
  constraint x2A + x2B == 1;
  constraint x3A + x3B == 1;
  cA <- 2*x1A + 3*x2A + 4*x3A;
  cB <- 2*x1B + 3*x2B + 4*x3B + 5;
  obj <- max(cA, cB);
  minimize obj;}
```

The LSP modeling framework includes five predefined functions: `input()`, `model()`, `param()`, `display()`, and `output()`. These functions have the following use:

- `input`: to declare the problem data or read data files.
- `model`: to declare the optimization model.
- `param`: to set parameter values before running the search.

- `display`: to display statistics or information in console or files during the search.
- `output`: to write results in console or files once the search is completed.

LocalSolver executes the functions in the order given above. The `model()` function is the only one that must be included in an LSP model, the other four are optional. The `model()` function for Example 5.3 starts with the definition of the six decision variables as binary, or Boolean as they are referred to in LSP. The left arrow, called the "link" operator, is used to define a LocalSolver (LS) Expression. These are the only expressions that are passed to the solver. In other words, any other variable or expression that is not defined this way could be used for intermediate calculations but the solver is not aware of them. The three assignment constraints are specified using the "constraint" keyword. The keyword indicates that the equation that follows should be treated as problem constraint. The objective function in the LSP model differs from the mathematical programming model shown above. Two LS expressions are defined, one for each machine. The expressions calculate the completion times `cA` and `cB` for machines A and B, respectively. The objective function to be minimized is defined as the maximum of the two completion times.

The file *Example 5.3.lsp* contains the LSP model for Example 5.3 including an `output()` function that displays the best solution found. The command line to execute LocalSolver on the Example 5.3 LSP model is:

```
localsolver Example5.3.lsp lsTimeLimit=1
```

In order to execute this command line, LocalSolver must be downloaded and installed. In this command line, the search parameter `lsTimeLimit` is set to 1, indicating that the search should stop after one second . Given the size of the problem, one second is more than sufficient to find the optimal solution. The output of the run is:

```
Objective function value: 7
Machine A: 2 3
Machine B: 1
```

While there are sophisticated ways of integrating LocalSolver with Excel, these forms of integration (e.g., through a .NET framework) require programming skills and knowledge of the Windows operating system that are beyond the scope of this book. A low level integration can be achieved using the `Shell` function in VBA. This function runs an executable program with the specified parameters.

5.2.1 Binary Optimization Problems

The following example illustrates the process of linking a spreadsheet model with a LSP model to solve a binary optimization problem with LocalSolver. The relevant files for this example are *Example5.4.xlsx* and *Example5.4.lsp*.

Example 5.4 Consider the assignment problem described in Example 5.2. We want to develop a LSP model to use LocalSolver to find a high quality solution to this problem. Decisions will be represented by binary variables. The problem data will be written in a text file named *Example5.4.dat*. At termination, LocalSolver will be instructed to write an output file named *Example5.4.out* that will contain the best solution found.

For the purpose of this example, it is assumed that the data file (named *Example 5.4.dat*) is structured as follows:

Number of facilities
Number of customers
Revenue values
Resource requirements
Demand
Capacity
Cost

Given this structure, the LSP `input()` function takes on the following form:

```
function input()
{
    dataFile = io.openRead("Example5.4.dat");
    facilities = dataFile.readInt();
    customers = dataFile.readInt();
    revenue[i in 1..facilities][j in 1..customers] = dataFile.readInt();
    resources[i in 1..facilities][j in 1..customers] = dataFile.readInt();
    demand[i in 1..facilities][j in 1..customers] = dataFile.readInt();
    capacity[i in 1..facilities] = dataFile.readInt();
    cost[i in 1..facilities] = dataFile.readInt();
    dataFile.close();
}
```

The first two values, i.e., number of facilities and number of customers, determine the size of the problem. These values are used to set the dimension of the arrays that store all the relevant problem data. LSP allows for a very compact way of dimensioning arrays at the same time that the data values are read from the file. Only one line of code is needed per array. The data arrays are used to formulate the problem with the following `model()` function:

```
function model()
{
// x[i][j] = 1 if customer i assigned to facility j and 0 otherwise
x[i in 1..facilities][j in 1..customers] <- bool();

// resource capacity should not be exceeded
for[i in 1..facilities]
constraint sum[j in 1..customers] (resources[i][j]*x[i][j]) <= capacity[i];

// customers must be assigned to one facility
for[j in 1..customers]
```

```
constraint sum[i in 1..facilities] (x[i][j]) == 1;

// objective function is profit
totalrevenue <- sum[i in 1..facilities][j in 1..customers]
(revenue[i][j]*x[i][j]);
for[i in 1..facilities]
sqrtdemand[i] <- sqrt(sum[j in 1..customers] (demand[i][j]*x[i][j]));
totalcost <- sum[i in 1..facilities] (cost[i]*sqrtdemand[i]);
profit <- totalrevenue - totalcost;
maximize profit;
}
```

This function includes comments, the lines starting with two forward slashes. The binary decision variables are defined first. In LSP, this definition is done with the `bool()` function, where bool stands for Boolean. Next, the constraints of the problem are declared, starting with the capacity constraints. There is one constraint per facility and hence the need for the for-loop. The left hand side of the constraint is the sum of the product between the resources and the assignment variables. The right hand side of the constraint is the capacity value for the corresponding facility. The form in which this constraint is declared follows very closely its mathematical programming formulation. There is one assignment constraint per customer and they are formulated as the sum of the assignment variables over all facilities. The final section of the model function formulates the objective function, which is given by the total profit. Total revenues are calculated first as the sum of the product between the revenue values and the assignment variables. Then, the square root of the total demand in each facility is calculated. The total demand is simply the sum of the product between the demand values and the assignment variables. The total cost is the sum of the product between the cost at each facility and the square root of the total demand at the facility. Finally, the profit is the difference between total revenue and total cost. The last line in the function indicates that the profit must be maximized.

The `output()` function is the last piece of the LSP file. The function is configured to create an output file with the assignments corresponding to the best solution found. The LSP instructions to create that *Example5.4.out* file are:

```
function output()
{
    outputFile = io.openWrite("Example5.4.out");
    for[i in 1..facilities] {
        for[j in 1..customers]
            outputFile.print(" " + getValue(x[i][j]));
        outputFile.println();
    }
    outputFile.close();
}
```

The *Example5.4.xlsx* workbook contains a spreadsheet model of the problem and a VBA Module called RunLocalSolver that contains the Sub procedure that calls

LocalSolver. (It is recommended that the VBA Module be loaded in order to follow the rest of this discussion.) At the top of the VBA module there is a declaration of three functions that are used to control the execution of the `Shell` function. These functions are needed because VBA does not "wait" for the process (in this case, LocalSolver) called by `Shell` to finish. Clearly, we need LocalSolver to finish first before we can read the output file that it generates. The LocalSolver Sub procedure starts with creating the "*Example5.4.dat*" file. This file has the structure indicated above, using the data values currently in the spreadsheet model. Then, the `Shell` function is used to invoke LocalSolver, as follows:

```
Shell ("localsolver Example5.4.lsp lsTimeLimit=2")
```

This assumes that LocalSolver has been installed and that the current directory to which Excel is pointing contains the `Example5.4.lsp` file. The time limit is set to 2 s. After the completion of the execution of the LocalSolver, the `Example5.4.out` is created. The VBA Module then opens the file, reads the solution, and inserts the values in cells `B6:U10` of the spreadsheet model. The solution found by LocalSolver has a revenue of 422, a cost of 198.41, and a profit of 223.59. Table 5.5 summarizes the models solutions obtained by the two solvers that have been employed so far.

Table 5.5 Summary of models and results for Examples 5.2 and 5.4

Solution representation	Constraints	Solver	Best solution
Binary	All	Evolutionary	Infeasible
Discrete value	Capacity	Evolutionary	Infeasible
Discrete value	None	Evolutionary	220.22
Binary	All	LocalSolver	223.59

The results in the first two rows of Table 5.5 point out the limitations of Excel's Evolutionary Solver when tackling constrained optimization problems. These limitations were somewhat overcome by changing the solution representation and by absorbing all constraints within the black-box evaluator. The result is shown in the third row of Table 5.5. LocalSolver, on the other hand, is well-equipped to dealing with constraints, particularly when the natural solution representation of the decisions in the problem is a set of binary variables.

5.2.2 *Optimization Problems on Permutations*

As discussed in Chap. 2, permutations are useful solution representations. Permutations are used both as direct and as indirect representations. The following example is introduced to illustrate how permutation problems (i.e., optimization problems with solutions representations given by a permutation) can be tackled with both Excels Evolutionary Solver and LocalSolver.

Example 5.5 A production facility must process jobs on a single machine. Each job j has a known processing time $t(j)$ and a known delay penalty $p(j)$, which is charged for every unit of time that the start of the job is delayed from the beginning of processing (that is, time zero). Therefore, the first job in the sequence is the only one that does not pay any delay costs. There is also a setup cost $c(i, j)$ that must be paid to change the machine from job i to job j. Tables 5.6 and 5.7 show the data corresponding to a small instance of this problem with 5 jobs.

Table 5.6 Processing times and delay penalties for small single-machine sequencing problem

Job	1	2	3	4	5
Processing time	3	4	1	4	5
Delay penalty	700	800	100	300	200

Table 5.7 Set up costs for small single-machine sequencing problem

Job	Job					
	1	2	3	4	5	6
0	1100	600	1200	2000	1400	
1		1300	700	1200	1100	1000
2	900		1100	1300	600	1200
3	900	1000		2000	700	1500
4	1000	700	800		600	1200
5	1400	1300	1200	1300		90

The setup costs in Table 5.7 include two extra jobs, 0 and 6, with zero processing time and zero delay penalty. The cost from job 0 to any other job (except job 6) is considered an initial setup to start the production. The cost from any job (except job 0) to job 6 is considered a cleanup cost at the end of the production process. The solution to this problem can be represented by permutation (i.e., sequence) variables s, where s_j represents the job in the jth position. For a problem with n jobs, $n+2$ variables are needed with $s_0 = 0$ and $s_{n+1} = n+1$. Since the values of the first and last variables are fixed, the optimization problem consists of finding the values of the s_j variables for which $j = 1, \ldots, n$. The restrictions are:

$$1 \leq s_j \leq n$$
$$s \text{ are all different}$$

The objective function is calculated as follows:

$$f(s) = \sum_{j=2}^{n} d(j)p(s_j) + \sum_{j=1}^{n+1} c(s_{j-1}, s_j)$$

$$d(j) = \sum_{i=1}^{j-1} t(s_i) \quad j = 2, \ldots, n$$

The value of $d(j)$ represents the delay of the start of the job in position j. Since the job in the first position starts immediately, its delay is zero. The delay of the job in the second position is the processing time of the job in the first position. The delay of the jobs in all the positions after that is simply the sum of all the processing times in earlier positions. The optimal solution to the small 5-job problem in Tables 5.6 and 5.7 is the following:

$$(0, 2, 1, 4, 3, 5, 6)$$

The objective function value corresponding to this solution is:

$$f = 4 * 700 + 7 * 300 + 11 * 100 + 12 * 200 + 600 + 900 + \\ + 1200 + 800 + 700 + 900 = 13,500$$

This 5-job problem has 120 unique solutions, which correspond to the number of permutations of 5 objects. (Recall that both job 0 and job 6 are fixed at each end of the sequence.) So, it would be relatively simple to enumerate all possibilities. Consider, however, the data in the file *Example5.5.xlsx*. There are two tabs in the workbook, Solution and Setup. The Solution worksheet includes the process time and the delay penalty data for a problem instance with 100 jobs. The Sequence column is the solution to the problem, indicating the order in which the jobs will be processed. Then the objective function is calculated as the sum of the delay costs and the setup cost. The Setup worksheet contains the setup cost matrix.

The problem is formulated to be solved using both Excel's Evolutionary Solver and LocalSolver. Figure 5.3 shows the optimization model for the Evolutionary Solver.

TotalCost in Fig. 5.3 is cell `K7`, which contains the sum of the delay and the setup costs. Cells `E6:E105` are defined as the Sequence and are the changing cells in the model. The restrictions indicate that the decision variable values (i.e., the changing cells) must be between 1 and the total number of jobs, and they also have to be all different in order to represent a permutation. The initial solution is given as the

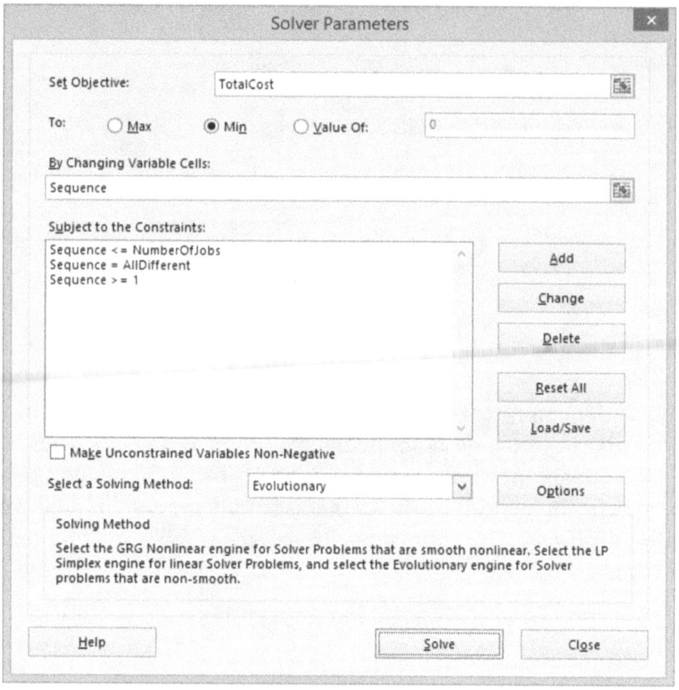

Fig. 5.3 Example 5.5 optimization model for the Evolutionary Solver

sequence of the jobs ordered by their job number. This solution has a total cost of 157,455, with 54,662 of delay cost and 102,793 of setup cost. The best solution found by the Evolutionary Solver has a total cost of 122,750 (56,844 of delay cost and 65,906 of setup cost).

The *Example5.5.lsp* file contains the LocalSolver model for this problem, consisting of `input()`, `model()`, and `output()` functions. The `input()` and `output()` functions are self-explanatory. They are designed, respectively, to read the problem data from a text file and to create an output file (also text) with the best sequence found during the search. The `model()` function has the following form:

```
function model() {
// Define a list variable where jobs[i] is the index of the ith job in the
sequence
jobs <- list(nJobs);

// All jobs must be in the sequence
constraint count(jobs) == nJobs;

// Calculate delay cost
delay[1] <- ptime[jobs[0]];
delay[j in 2..nJobs-1] <- delay[j-1] + ptime[jobs[j-1]];
delayCost <- sum[j in 1..nJobs-1] (delay[j]*penalty[jobs[j]]);

// Calculate setup cost
```

```
setupCost <- setup[0][jobs[0]] + setup[jobs[nJobs-1]+1][nJobs];
setupCost <- setupCost + sum[i in 1..nJobs-1] (setup[jobs[i-1]+1][jobs[i]]);

// Calculate objective function
obj <- delayCost + setupCost;
minimize obj;
}
```

As mentioned above, LocalSolver includes a special type of variables called `list`. This type of variables is particularly useful to model sequencing problems. For this problem, we define a single list containing the index of the jobs. The first index value in a `list` is zero and therefore the job indices in the LSP range from 0 to $n - 1$. The calculation of the delay cost and the setup cost is adjusted to take into consideration that both the job indices and the indices of the arrays containing the processing time (`ptime`), the delay penalty (`penalty`), and the setup cost (`setup`) also start from zero. Note that the delays are calculated recursively, generating a compact formulation with only n LS expressions.

The *Example5.5.xlsx* workbook includes a VBA module similar to the one described above for Example 5.4. The module creates the data file, calls LocalSolver, and reads the output to display the solution in Solution worksheet. The time that the Local Solver is instructed to run is specified in cell `L10` of the Solution worksheet. This cell is used by the VBA code as follows:

```
commandLine = "cmd.exe /c localsolver Example5.5.lsp
   fileName=Example5.5 _lsTimeLimit =" +
   CStr(Worksheets("Solution").Cells(10, 12).Value)
procID = Shell(commandLine, vbNormalFocus)
```

The command line calls the Windows Console application (i.e., `cmd.exe`) and instructs it to run `localsolver` with the specified arguments. The "`/c`" option instructs the console to close after termination. The `vbNormalFocus` argument value for the `Shell` function indicates that the console should be visible during the execution. This is done because the problem with 100 jobs is large and it requires at least 30 s of search to find high quality solutions. The Console application allows the monitoring of the progress of the search during the execution of the LocalSolver.

Executing the LocalSolver for 60 s, which is about one third of the time that the Evolutionary Solver required to find the solution reported above, results in a solution with a total cost of 108,954 (52,139 of delay cost and 56,815 of setup cost). The best solution found by the Evolutionary Solver is 12.7% more costly than the solution found by the LocalSolver. If LocalSolver is allowed to run for 180 s, a run-time that is equivalent to the Evolutionary Solver, a slightly improved solution with a total cost of 108,497 is found.

All the examples in this section focused on the general-purpose LocalSolver. There is also a black-box LocalSolver than can be used in situations where the complexity of modeling the evaluation function goes beyond what can accomplished with LSP. For instance, an Excel spreadsheet could be the black-box function to be optimized by LocalSolver. This can be accomplished by the .NET C# version of

LocalSolver. However, the level of programming required to assemble such a system is outside the scope of this book.

5.3 OptQuest

While LocalSolver is a general-purpose optimizer that is based on a single-solution search, most black-box optimizers are built on population-based frameworks. Excels Evolutionary Solver is one example of such a system. As the name indicates, the population-based methodology that is behind Excels metaheuristic solver falls within the family of evolutionary computation methods. In specific, the solver is an implementation of a genetic algorithm. Another popular black-box optimization engine, known as OptQuest,[3] also operates on population of solutions in order to search for high quality solutions to optimization problems. In contrast to all other commercial black-box optimizers, OptQuest's main search engine follows the principles of the scatter search methodology.

Like other black-box solvers, OptQuest is not totally "ignorant" of the problem context because the selection of the solution representation gives some information to the optimization engine. OptQuest allows users to represent solutions as a mixture of continuous, discrete, integer, binary, permutation, and other specialized variables (such as, project, categorical, or enumeration). Clearly, the solution representation gives OptQuest some information about the problem context and therefore the solver context-independence changes with each particular application because the amount of information that it receives varies. OptQuest chooses specific solvers based on the characteristics of the optimization model: pure or mixed, constrained or unconstrained and deterministic or stochastic.

While scatter search continues to be the main methodology within OptQuest, other technologies both for prediction and for optimization have been added to the system. Search options and settings alter the behavior of the solution process in order to tackle difficult problems. Since OptQuest is built under the assumption that a computationally expensive black box is used to evaluate the objective function of the optimization problem being solved, prediction models within the engine have the dual purpose of assisting in establishing search directions as well as estimating the value of the objective function before solutions are processed by the objective function evaluator.

The OptQuest engine follows an object-oriented programming structure. There are two key tasks for the user:

1. Define the optimization model (i.e., decision variables and constraints).
2. Provide an objective function evaluator (i.e., the black box).

[3] OptQuest is a product of OptTek Systems (http://opttek.com). The OptQuest COM interface and an academic license to run the examples presented in this section can be requested by sending email to optinfo@opttek.com.

The objective function evaluator could range in complexity from a simple equation to a computer simulation. The evaluator is called every time that the search generates a solution for which it wants to know its objective function value. OptQuest is a fairly complex system and a deep exploration of its functionality is beyond the scope of this book. The following two examples illustrate the general structure of the COM version of OptQuest and some of the key features.

Example 5.6 Consider the assignment problem described in Example 5.2. Develop an OptQuest model to find a high quality solution to this problem. Decision are represented by binary variables and the optimization model within OptQuest includes both cover and resource constraints. A spreadsheet model evaluates the objective function for each solution generated by the OptQuest search.

The OptQuest COM interface enables the use of the OptQuest search engine from Excel VBA. A Module and Class Module must be added to the VBA project, as shown the *Example5.6.xlsm* file. The OptQuest Module contains the OptQuestSolver Sub needed to set up the optimize model in OptQuest and the OptQuestListener Class Module contains the Evaluate Event Sub. The relevant functions in the OptQuestSolver Sub are:

- `AddUserControlledObjective`: to declare the objective function is a black box controlled by the user.
- `AddBinaryVariable`: to define the decision variables.
- `AddEQConstraint`: to add the cover constraints.
- `AddLEConstraint`: to add the resource capacity constraints.
- `SetMaximumTime`: to set the optimization time.
- `Optimize`: to instruct OptQuest to search.
- `GetBestSolution`: to retrieve the best solution found during the search.

During the search, the Evaluate Event Sub procedure is the main communication between OptQuest and the user-controlled objective function. i.e., the black box. The OptQuest engine generates solutions that conform to the optimization model, in this case, it produces the values for 100 binary variables that satisfy both the cover and resource constraints. These variable values are then put in the appropriate cells in the spreadsheet model and the resulting profit value is passed back to the OptQuest engine. The main OpQuest functions are:

- `GetSolutionVariableValue`: to retrieve the values of the decision variables from OptQuest.
- `SetSolutionObjectiveValue`: to pass the value of the objective function value to OptQuest.
- `EvaluateComplete`: to instruct OptQuest that the evaluation has been completed.

When the optimization is executed with a time limit of 45 s, OptQuest matches the best-known solution for this problem that has a total profit of 223.59. There is a noticeable difference between the time needed by OptQuest to find the best solution and the time needed by LocalSolver (approximately 2 s on the same computer equipment). This is due to the search strategies used by each procedure. OptQuest is built to minimize the number of calls to the black box evaluator because its main application is in the area of expensive black boxes. An expensive black box is one for which the calculation of the objective function requires a significant amount of computer effort. A computer simulation is a good example of an expensive black box. A system that is set up to optimize expensive black boxes spends considerable time making decisions about what solution to evaluate next. LocalSolver, on the other hand, assumes that the objective function value can be obtained quickly. Therefore, it generates and evaluates thousands of solutions in a fraction of a second. The end result is that, for the same amount of computer effort, a system like LocalSolver performs better than a system like OptQuest when the objective function evaluation is computationally inexpensive. And, the opposite is generally true for expensive black boxes. In this particular example, it is difficult to compare the performance based on speed because LocalSolver has some knowledge of the objective function that is modeled in LSP with LS expressions. In addition, the way LocalSolver is called, it has no interaction with the spreadsheet model during the search. In contrast, OptQuest has no knowledge of the mathematical form of the objective function and the evaluation requires the recalculation of the spreadsheet model for each trial solution that the search generates.

Example 5.7 Consider the sequencing problem described in Example 5.5. Develop an OptQuest model to find a high quality solution to this problem. Decision are represented by permutation variables defined within OptQuest. A spreadsheet model evaluates the objective function for each solution generated by the OptQuest search.

The structure to apply OptQuest to this problem is similar to the one used for Example 5.6. The *Example5.7.xlsm* file contains the spreadsheet model and the related VBA modules (OptQuest and OptQuestListener). In this case, the decision variables are declared with the `AddPermutationVariable` method. There is no need for constraints since the variable definition implicitly enforces that all values must be different. A 180 s execution results in a solution with an objective function value of 175,914, which is considerably worse than the solution found with LocalSolver. This result is consistent with the observation made above. That is, OptQuest is designed to optimize expensive black boxes that have a relatively small number of variables and where the main goal is to find solutions of acceptable quality with a limited number of calls to the objective function evaluator.

5.4 Predictive Analytics: Clustering Analysis

Cluster analysis or clustering consists of mutually exclusive grouping a set of elements in such a way that elements in the same group (also referred to as a cluster) are more similar (by some metric) to each other than to those in other clusters. Clustering is one of the main exploratory tools in data mining, and a common technique for statistical data analysis, used in many fields, including marketing.

Cluster analysis is a concept that can be approached in several ways by multiple algorithms that apply different meanings as to what constitutes a cluster. Due to the variety of ways in which dissimilarity of the elements can be measured and the different forms in which these measure can be used to computing the merit of a particular configuration, clustering has been formulated as a multi-objective optimization problem (see for example [2]). The typical data associated with a clustering problem consist of a set of n records (elements), each one consisting of d attributes. Let a_{ij} be the value of the jth attribute of element i in the data set. Using these data, a very common model is one in which, given a fixed number of clusters k, the problem is to find the assignment of the n elements to the k clusters that minimizes the sum of the squared Euclidean distances between each point and its assigned cluster centroid.

Suppose that S_k is the set of elements assigned to cluster k. Then each attribute c_{kj} of the centroid $c_k = (c_{k1}, \ldots, c_{kd})$ of cluster k is calculated as follows:

$$c_{kj} = \frac{\sum\limits_{i \in S_k}}{|S_k|} a_i ij$$

In other words, the centroid of a cluster is the average of the attribute values associated with the elements assigned to the cluster. In the formula above, $|S_k|$ denotes the cardinality of (i.e., the number of elements in) set S_k. The sum in the numerator is over all the attribute values corresponding to elements assigned to cluster k. The centroids form the basis for the objective function calculation that measures the merit of a particular clustering S:

$$f(S) = \sum_{l=1}^{k} \sum_{i \in S_l} \sum_{j=1}^{d} (a_{ij} - c_{kj})^2$$

k-Means is the best-known heuristic to find solutions to this problem. The procedure is summarized as follows:

1. Choose k cluster centroids.
2. Assign each element to the closest cluster, where distance to the cluster is measured to the cluster centroid. That is, element i should be assigned to the cluster k for which $\sum\limits_{j=1}^{d} (a_{ij} - c_{kj})^2$ is minimized.
3. Recalculate the centroids employing the current cluster membership.
4. If convergence criteria are satisfied then stop, otherwise return to step 2.

Several strategies are used to perform the first step. For instance, the centroids could be chosen at random within the domain defined by all the elements in the problem. Systematic procedures attempt to choose centroids that are significantly different among themselves. The convergence criteria in step 4 typically includes some form of metric to determine if the centroids have changed from one iteration to the next. A hard stop is also possible to make sure that the procedure terminates if it reaches some maximum number of iterations.

Example 5.8 Consider the data in Table 5.8. Apply the *k*-means heuristic to find an assignment of the 7 elements into two clusters.

Table 5.8 Data for clustering Example 5.8

Elements	Attribute 1	Attribute 2
1	1.0	1.0
2	1.5	2.0
3	3.0	4.0
4	5.0	7.0
5	3.5	5.0
6	4.5	5.0
7	3.5	4.5

For the initial centroids, the elements that are farthest apart from each other are chosen. It can be easily verified that elements 1 and 4 are the most distant from each other. Therefore, centroid 1 is (1.0, 1.0) and centroid 2 is (5.0, and 7.0). In step 2, the squared distance from each element to each centroid is calculated in order to determine the assignment of the 5 remaining elements. Table 5.9 shows these calculations.

Table 5.9 Initial squared distances to centroids

Elements	Squared distance to centroid 1	Squared distance to centroid 2
1	0.00	52.00
2	1.25	37.25
3	13.00	13.00
4	52.00	0.00
5	22.25	6.25
6	28.25	4.25
7	18.50	8.50

The calculations in Table 5.9 show that elements 1 and 2 should be assigned to cluster 1. Elements 5, 6, and 7 should be assigned to cluster 2. Element 3 is at the same squared distance from both clusters. Let us arbitrarily assign this element to cluster 1. The new centroids are:

$$c_1 = (1.833, 2.333)$$
$$c_2 = (4.125, 5.375)$$

Table 5.10 shows the updated squared distances, taking into consideration the new centroids shown above. The sum of the squared distances from elements 1, 2, and 3 to centroid 1 and the sum of the squared distances from elements 4, 5, 6, and 7 to centroid 2 is the value of the objective function value, which in this case totals 12.208.

Table 5.10 Squared distances to centroids after the first assignment

Elements	Squared distance to centroid 1	Squared distance to centroid 2
1	2.472	28.906
2	0.222	18.281
3	4.139	3.156
4	31.806	3.406
5	9.889	0.531
6	14.222	0.281
7	7.472	1.156

After the recalculation of the squared distances considering the new centroids, it becomes evident that element 3 should be switched to cluster 2. (Note that in Table 5.10 the squared distances from element 3 to clusters 1 and 2 are 4.139 and 3.156, respectively.) Once this switch is made, the new centroids have the following values:

$$c_1 = (1.25, 1.50)$$
$$c_2 = (3.90, 5.10)$$

It can now be verified that all elements are assigned to their nearest cluster. The objective function value associated with this solution is 8.525.

This clustering problem can be formulated as a nonlinear binary mathematical program. Let x_{il} be a binary variable that takes on a value of one if element i is assigned to cluster l. Then, the following is a mathematical programming formulation of the problem:

$$
\begin{aligned}
\min \quad & \sum_{l=1}^{k}\sum_{i=1}^{n} x_{il}\left(\sum_{j=1}^{d}(a_{ij}-c_{lj})^2\right) \\
& c_{lj} = \frac{\sum_{i=1}^{n} x_{il}a_{ij}}{\sum_{i=1}^{n} x_{il}} \\
\text{subject to} \quad & \sum_{l=1}^{k} x_{il} = 1 \quad \text{for } i = 1,\dots,n \\
& \sum_{l=1}^{n} x_{il} \geq 1 \quad \text{for } l = 1,\dots,k \\
& x_{ij} = \{0,1\}
\end{aligned}
$$

The objective function is the sum of the squared distances from each element to its cluster centroid. Cluster centroids are calculated as the average attribute value for all the elements assigned to the cluster. The first set of constrains indicate that an element can only be assigned to one cluster. The second set of constraints force that at least one element is assigned to each cluster. This guarantees that the elements are assigned to exactly k clusters.

This mathematical program is very difficult to solve by conventional methods because of the form of the objective function and the potentially large number of binary variables. However, a black-box metaheuristic optimizer such as LocalSolver is able to find high-quality solutions to this difficult problem. The *Clustering.lsp* file contains LSP code for the clustering problem, where the `model()` function takes on the following form:

```
function model(){
  // x[i][l] = 1 if element i is assigned to cluster l
  x[i in 1..n][l in 1..k] <- bool();

  // elements should be assigned to only one cluster
  for[i in 1..n]
    constraint sum[l in 1..k] (x[i][l]) == 1;

  // there should be exactly k clusters
  for[l in 1..k]
    constraint sum[i in 1..n] (x[i][l]) >= 1;

  // calculate centroids
  c[l in 1..k][j in 1..d] <- (sum[i in 1..n]
    (x[i][l]*a[i][j])) / sum[i in 1..n] (x[i][l]);

  // objective function
  obj <- sum[l in 1..k][i in 1..n] (x[i][l] *
         sum[j in 1..d] (pow(a[i][j]-c[l][j], 2)));
  minimize obj;
}
```

The function follows the format of the mathematical programming formulation. The input for this LSP is in Example5.8.dat. The following command line solves the problem with LocalSolver:

```
localsolver Clustering.lsp fileName=Example5.8 k=2 lsTimeLimit=2
```

LocalSolver is able to find the same solution as the k-means heuristic for the small dataset in Example 5.8. In the next section both k-means and the LocalSolver formulation of the clustering problem are applied to a marketing segmentation problem.

5.5 Case Studies

The previous chapters introduced several metaheuristic methodologies and applications. This chapter introduced the notion of black-box optimization and three optimizers have been described and applied. In an attempt to bring all these concepts together, the book concludes with two case studies. The first one is more a programming project than a typical case study appearing in a decision analytics book. The second is a marketing application that does have the flavor of a typical case study and that builds on the programming work from the first one.

5.5.1 GRASP and k-Means for Clustering

The k-Means method has been shown to be sensitive to the initial grouping. That is, the quality of the final clustering found with k-Means is highly dependent on the starting point. To overcome this shortcoming, most commercial applications of the procedure include options for generating several initial groupings from which to apply k-Means. Random partitions of the elements is the most common way of generating these starting points. As shown in Chap. 3, however, total randomness as a mechanism to generate diverse solution is seldom the best option. This section describes the design of a GRASP that uses k-Means as the improvement method to solve the clustering problem described above. The performance of the resulting procedure, which is clearly specialized to the clustering problem, is then compared to LocalSolver, which treats the problem as a black box.

Kaufmans heuristic is a greedy approach to clustering. It is based on selecting k elements in the set to represent the cluster centroids. The first element is the most centrally located. The remaining $k-1$ elements are selected sequentially according to a greedy rule. The rule identifies the element that has the largest potential of "attracting" more of the unassigned elements and that is as far as possible from the selected centroids. The most centrally located element is the one closest to the centroid of the data, given by $\bar{c} = (\bar{c}_1, \ldots, \bar{c}_d)$, where:

$$\bar{c}_j = \frac{\sum_{i=1}^{n} a_{ij}}{n}$$

The first centroid is the element i for which $\sum_{i=1}^{n} (a_{ij} - \bar{c}_j)^2$ is minimum. The element is added to the set S, which contains all the elements already chosen to represent the centroid of a cluster. For each of the elements that has not been selected as a centroid (i.e., that does not belong to the set S), the following greedy value is calculated:

$$g_i = \sum_{i' \notin S} \max\left(D_{i'} - \sum_{j=1}^{d} (a_{ij} - a_{i'j})^2, 0\right)$$

$$D_i = \max_{i' \in S}\left(\sum_{j=1}^{d} (a_{ij} - a_{i'j})^2\right)$$

D_i represents the squared distance between element i and the closest centroid already in S. The greedy function value for element i (i.e., g_i) accumulates, for all the elements i' that have not been chosen as centroids, all the positive differences between the squared distance to their preferred cluster (i.e., $D_{i'}$) and their squared distance to element i. A value of zero for the greedy function g_i indicates that the distance from all elements to one of the selected centroids is less than the distance to element i. In other words, if element i were selected as centroid, no element in the set would be assigned to the cluster represented by element i because they would preferred to be assigned to a cluster represented by one of the elements already in S. The larger the value of g_i the more attractive element i is to be selected as centroid. That is because a large value is achieved when both the element is away from current centroids and close to elements that have not been chosen as centroids.

Example 5.9 Apply the Kaufman heuristic to the data in Example 5.8.

The overall centroid is $\bar{c} = (3.143, 4.071)$. These values are obtained by simply averaging the second and third columns of Table 5.8. Element 3 is the closest to this centroid. Therefore, element 3 is chosen as the centroid that represents the first cluster. Table 5.11 shows the D and g values for all the elements, except element 3.

The second centroid is the one with the largest greedy function value. Hence, element 1 or 2 may be chosen to represent the second cluster. Suppose element 1 is selected. Then, a complete solution is obtained by assigning elements 2, 4, 5, 6, and 7 to their closest centroid. For this small example, the assignment results in the optimal solutions, where elements 1 and 2 belong to one cluster and the rest of the elements belong to the other.

Table 5.11 Greedy function values for elements in Example 5.9

Elements	D	g
1	13.00	18.00
2	6.25	18.00
4	13.00	13.00
5	1.25	10.50
6	3.25	12.25
7	0.50	8.00

The purpose of this case is to build a GRASP that uses a pseudo-randomized version of the Kaufman heuristic to construct solutions and k-Means to improve them. The *Online Retailer.xlsm* file contains a dataset and a VBA module with Sheldon Neilsons implementation of the k-Means heuristic.

1. Use the k-Means in the workbook to find a clustering of the data with $k = 3$.
2. Create a VBA module to code the Kaufman heuristic and to find a clustering of the data with $k = 3$. Compare the solution found with the Kaufman heuristic and the solution found in part 1 with k-Means.
3. Use the grouping found with the Kaufman procedure as a starting point for k-Means. Compare this solution with the two previously found.
4. Create a VBA module with a GRASP that combines the Kaufman heuristic and k-Means. Find the best value for the alpha parameter associated with the reduced candidate list. Determine a number of GRASP iterations that result in a good performance of the procedure. Compare the solution found with the fine-tuned procedure with all the other solutions found so far.
5. Apply the *Clustering.lsp* LocalSolver model to this problem. Choose a time limit that is equivalent to the running time of the fine-tuned GRASP. Compare the solutions found with GRASP and LocalSolver.
6. Comment on the amount of effort involved in coding the components of GRASP and the gain in the solution quality (if any) with respect to the solution found with LocalSolver.

5.5.2 *Marketing Segmentation: Deal Proneness Across Sales Promotion Types*[4]

Sales promotions constitute a large portion of the promotional budgets for packaged goods manufacturers. Often, packaged goods manufacturers spending on consumer sales promotions exceeds that spent on advertising. Firms average using more than eight types of consumer sales promotion. Firms are therefore interested in studying the consumer response to promotion techniques. In particular, firms would like to know whether there is a segment of consumers that is consistently "prone" to deals across different sales promotion types or, given some conceptual differences across deal types, multiple consumer segments exist at more deal-specific level.

This segmentation issue is relevant to firms that employ multiple types of consumer sales promotions and are interested in more effectively targeting their promotions at specific consumer segments. Tactical questions involving the use of different types of deals by a segment have some similarities to the development of advertising schedules that focus on reach (i.e., the percentage of consumers exposed to an ad) and frequency (i.e., the number of times the consumer is exposed to the ad). For example, if consumers are prone only to specific deal types (e.g., a coupon prone segment; a display prone segment), to obtain effective reach among these consumers it would be necessary for companies to use many different sales promotion techniques, each targeted at a different segment. However, if there is overlap in proneness so that a consumer segment is prone across different deal types, it becomes more efficient to reach these consumers using a less diverse set of promotional vehicles. Given that packaged goods manufacturers average use of more than eight types of sales promotion, and firms use of new types of promotions has increased, such questions are highly relevant to retailers and marketers. These issues are increasing in importance due to marketers concern with better integration of marketing communications and the development of big data systems for more accurate targeting of promotions at consumers.

Some studies use scanner panel data to examine segmentation-related questions for sales promotions. Scanner panel studies infer a consumer proneness from purchase behaviors. A more direct approach consists of a three step process: (1) using multi-item measures to assess proneness to each of eight sales promotion types (coupon proneness, display proneness), (2) employing these proneness measures as the basis for determining segments of consumers, and (3) assessing relationships between proneness segments and marketplace purchase behaviors.

The study tests the following alternatives:

1. Given different sensitivities to sales promotion types, the market should be segmented according to consumer proneness to each deal type (a coupon prone segment, a rebate prone segment, etc.).

[4]Based on Lichtenstein, D.R., S. Burton and R.G. Netemeyer (1997) "An Examination of Deal Proneness Across Sales Promotion Types: A Consumer Segmentation Perspective," Journal of Retailing, vol. 73, no. 2, pp. 283-297.

2. There is sufficient similarity across sales promotion types to justify segmenting the consumer market across different deal types (a general deal prone segment, a deal insensitive segment).

The study included the following eight consumer deal proneness types: (1) proneness toward coupons, (2) sales, (3) cents-off, (4) buy-one-get-one-free, (5) free-gift-with-purchase, (6) end-of-aisle displays, (7) rebates/refunds, and (8) contests/sweepstakes. Shoppers were contacted by trained interviewers as they were exiting from two grocery stores (belonging to the same chain) and asked for their participation in a university-sponsored project concerning shopping attitudes and how people shop. Those agreeing to participate were asked to provide interviewers with their scanner-based grocery receipts and also were given a self-administered survey (to be answered at home and returned in a postage paid return envelope) and coupons from a local bakery that served as an inducement for participation. The take-home survey included (1) the multi-item measures of the eight deal-specific proneness types, (2) a seven-place scale pertaining to the frequency of grocery store coupon-redemption behavior and two open-ended questions which assessed the frequency of acting on rebate/refund and contests/sweepstakes offers, and (3) socioeconomic and demographic measures. Data from returned surveys were merged with the scanner-based purchase behavior information coded from the grocery store receipt.

The data in Deal *Proneness.xlsm* shows the records for 524 respondents. The multi-item measures included the number of items for each deal type shown in Table 5.12.

Table 5.12 Number of items per deal type

Deal type	Number of items
Buy-one-get-one-free	6
Sales	6
Coupons	5
Cents-off	7
Free gift	6
In-store displays	7
Rebates	6
Contests/sweepstakes	6

All items were measured on seven point scales anchored by "Strongly Disagree" and "Strongly Agree." Therefore, the minimum score is the number of items (e.g., 5 for coupons) and the maximum score is the number of items times seven (e.g., 35 for coupons). The data in *Deal Proneness.xlsm* also includes four deal-responsive dependent variables: (1) coupon usage, (2) response to contests/sweepstakes, (3) response to rebate offers, and (4) end-of-aisle display purchases. (These columns include some blank cells, indicating missing data.)

The deal-responsive dependent variables are used to validate the results of the different clustering schemes. In particular, the dependent variables are helpful in identifying whether or not there are significant differences in deal proneness among customers in different clusters.

1. Use the best method identified in Sect. 5.5.1 to cluster customers in 2, 3, and 4 clusters.
2. Construct a table to compare the average values for each deal type and cluster in each of the clustering schemes (see *Cluster Analysis 1* tab).
3. Construct a table to compare the average values for each dependent variable and cluster in each of the clustering schemes (see *Cluster Analysis 2* tab).
4. What can you conclude from the values in the cluster analysis tables? Which alternative is supported by the cluster analyses?

References

1. Adenso-Díaz, B., and M. Laguna. 2006. Fine-tuning of algorithms using partial experimental designs and local search. *Operations Research* 54 (1): 99–114.
2. Caballero, R., M. Laguna, R. Martí, and J. Molina. 2011. Scatter tabu search for multiobjective clustering problems. *Journal of the Operational Research Society* 62: 2034–2046.
3. Cano, J.R., O. Cordón, F. Herrera, and L. Sánchez. 2002. A greedy randomized adaptive search procedure applied to the clustering problem as an initialization process using K-means as a local search procedure. *Journal of Intelligent and Fuzzy Systems* 12: 235–242.
4. Gonçalves, J.F., and M.G.C. Resende. 2011. Biased random-key genetic algorithms for combinatorial optimization. *Journal of Heuristics* 17 (5): 487–525.
5. Hoos, H.H. 2012. Programming by optimization. *Communications of the ACM* 55 (2): 70–80.
6. Laguna, M., and R. Martí. 2003. *Scatter search: methodology and implementations in C.* Berlin: Springer (2003).
7. Laguna, M., J. Molina, F. Pérez, R. Caballero, and A. Hernández-Díaz. 2010. The challenge of optimizing expensive black boxes: A scatter search/rough set theory approach. *Journal of the Operational Research Society* 61 (1): 53–67.
8. Ragsdale, C. 2015. *Spreadsheet modeling and decision analysis: A practical introduction to business analytics.* Boston: Cengage Learning.
9. Talbi, E-G. 2009. *Metaheuristics: From design to implementation.* New York: Wiley.

FSC
www.fsc.org
MIX
Papier | Fördert gute Waldnutzung
FSC® C083411

Kolibri 360 GmbH
Ferdinand-Jühlke-Straße 7
99095 Erfurt, Deutschland
produktsicherheit@kolibri360.de